A
MEDITATIVE
COMMENTARY
ON THE
NEW TESTAMENT

EPHESIANS, PHILIPPIANS, COLOSSIANS AND PHILEMON: JESUS ABOVE ALL

A
MEDITATIVE
COMMENTARY
ON THE
NEW TESTAMENT

EPHESIANS, PHILIPPIANS, COLOSSIANS AND PHILEMON: JESUS ABOVE ALL

By Earl Lavender

LEAFWOOD
PUBLISHERS

EPHESIANS, PHILIPPIANS, COLOSSIANS AND PHILEMON:
Jesus Above All

LEAFWOOD
P U B L I S H E R S

Copyright 2009 by Earl Lavender

ISBN 978-0-89112-561-7

Printed in the United States of America

Cover design by Greg Jackson, Thinkpen Design, LLC

For information contact:
Leafwood Publishers, Abilene, Texas
1-877-816-4455 toll free
www.leafwoodpublishers.com

08 09 10 11 12 13 / 7 6 5 4 3 2 1

To Leonard Allen, with deep gratitude for all you have done and continue to do for the expansion of God's kingdom

ACKNOWLEDGEMENTS

I am deeply thankful to Gary Holloway for partnering with me in this effort. His work in this series is outstanding. Not only is Gary a great writer, but a skilled and patient editor. His spiritual support and quality editing have been indispensable.

Sincere thanks to the Donelson family of faith for helping me develop these studies for their use. These brothers and sisters stand as a great example of a church committed to the daily study of God's word.

I would also like to offer a special word of thanks to the "early birds" who have for many years so diligently studied the word of God with me every Sunday morning at 7 a.m. If you are ever in Nashville on Sunday, please come and visit. These precious saints will change your life as they have mine.

None of this work could be done without the wonderful and loving support of Rebecca. She has taught me more than anyone else about living out the truth of Scripture. Besides Jesus, she is my greatest blessing in this life. I will be forever in her debt for her actively living in God's love as my spouse. She is my constant inspiration.

C O N T E N T S

COLOSSIANS

PHILEMON

HEARING GOD IN SCRIPTURE

There are many commentaries, guides, and workbooks on the various books of the Bible. How is this series different? It is not intended to answer all your scholarly questions about the Bible, or even make you an expert in the details of Scripture. Instead, this series is designed to help you hear the voice of God in your everyday life. It is a guide to meditation on the Bible, meditation that will allow the Bible to transform you.

We read in many ways. We might scan the newspaper for information, read a map for location, read a novel for pleasure, or read a textbook to pass a test. These are all good ways to read, depending on our circumstances.

A young soldier far away from home who receives a letter from his wife reads in yet another way. He might scan the letter quickly at first for news and information. But his longing for his beloved causes him to read the letter again and again, hearing her sweet voice in every line. He consciously treasures each word of this precious letter.

BIBLE STUDY

So also, there are many good ways to read the Bible, depending on our circumstances. Bible study is absolutely necessary for our life with God. We rightly study the Bible for information. We ask, "Who wrote this?" "When was it written?" "Who were the original readers?" "How do these words apply to me?" More importantly, we want information about God. Who is he? What does he think of me? What does he want from me?

There is no substitute for this kind of close, dedicated Bible study. We must know what the Bible says to know our standing with God. We therefore read the Bible to discover true doctrine or teaching. But some—in their emphasis on the authority and inspiration of the Bible—have forgotten that Bible study is not an end in itself. We want to know God through Scripture. We want to have a relationship with the Teacher, not just the teachings.

Jesus tells some of God's people in his day, "You diligently study the Scriptures because you think that by them you possess eternal life. These are the Scriptures that testify about me, yet you refuse to come to me to have life" (John 5:39-40). He's not telling them to study their Bibles less, but he is reminding them of the deeper purpose of Bible study—to draw us to God through Jesus. Bible study is a means, not an end.

Yet the way many of us have learned to study the Bible may actually get in the way of hearing God. "Bible study" may sound a lot like schoolwork, and many of us were happy to get out of school. "Bible study" may call to mind pictures of intellectuals surrounded by books in Greek and Hebrew, pondering meanings too deep for ordinary people. The method of Bible study that has been popular for some time focuses on the strangeness of the Bible. It was written long ago, far away, and in languages we cannot read. There is a huge gap between us and the original readers of the Bible, a gap that can only be bridged by scholars, not by average folk.

There is some truth and some value in that "scholarly" method. It is true that the Bible was not written originally to us. Knowing ancient languages and customs can at times help us understand the Bible better. However, one unintended result of this approach is to make the Bible distant from the people of God. We may come to think that we can only hear God indirectly through Scripture, that his word must be filtered through scholars. We may even think that deep Bible study is a matter of mastering obscure information about the Bible.

Meditation

But we read the Bible for more than information. By studying it, we experience transformation, the mysterious process of God at work in us. Through his loving words, God is calling us to life with him. He is forming us into the image of his Son.

Reading the Bible is not like reading other books. We are not simply trying to learn information or master material. Instead, we want to stand under the authority of Scripture and let God master us. While we read the Bible, it reads us, opening the depths of our being to the overpowering love of God. "For the word of God is living and active. Sharper than any double-edged sword, it penetrates even to dividing soul and spirit, joints and marrow; it judges the thoughts and attitudes of the heart. Nothing in all creation is hidden from God's sight. Everything is uncovered and laid bare before the eyes of him to whom we must give account" (Hebrews 4:12-13).

Opening our hearts to the word of God is meditation. Although this way of reading the Bible may be new to some, it has a long heritage among God's people. The Psalmist joyously meditates on the words of God (Psalm 1:2; 39:3; 119:15, 23, 27, 48, 78, 97, 99, 148). Meditation is taking the words of Scripture to heart and letting them ask questions of us. It is slowly chewing over a text, listening closely, reading God's message of love to us over and over. This is not a simple, easy, or naïve reading of Scripture, but a process that takes time, dedication, and practice on our part.

There are many ways to meditate on the Bible. One is praying the Scriptures. Prayer and Bible study really cannot be separated. One way of praying the Bible is to make the words of a text your prayer. Obviously, the prayer texts of Scripture, especially the Psalms, lend themselves to this. "The Lord is my shepherd" has been the prayer of many hearts.

It is proper and helpful to turn the words of the Bible into prayers. Commands from God can become prayers. "You shall have no other gods before me" (Exodus 20:3) can be prayed, "Lord, keep me from anything that takes your place in my heart." Stories can be prayed. Jesus heals a man born blind (John 9), and so we pray, "Lord Jesus open my eyes to who you truly are." Even the promises of the Bible become prayers. "Never will I leave you; never will I forsake you" (Deuteronomy 31:6; Hebrews 13:5) becomes "God help me know that you promise that you are always with me and so live my life without fear."

Obviously, there are many helpful ways of hearing the voice of God in Scripture. Again, the purpose of Bible reading and study is not to know more about the Bible, much less to pride ourselves as experts on Scripture. Instead, we read to hear the voice of our Beloved. We listen for a word from God to us.

Holy Reading

This commentary reflects one ancient way of meditation and praying the Scriptures known as lectio divina, or holy reading. This method assumes that God wants to speak to us directly in the Bible, that the passage we are reading is God's word to us right now. The writers of the New Testament read the Old Testament with this same conviction. They saw the words of the Bible speaking directly to their own situation. They read with humility and with prayer.

The first step along this way of holy reading is listening to the Bible. Choose a biblical text that is not too long. This commentary breaks Paul's prison epistles into smaller sections. The purpose is to hear God's voice in your current situation, not to cover material or prepare lessons. Get into a comfortable position and maintain silence before God for several minutes. This prepares the heart to listen. Read slowly. Savor each word. Perhaps read aloud. Listen for a particular phrase that speaks to you. Ask God, "What are you trying to tell me today?"

The next step is to meditate on that particular phrase. That meditation may include slowly repeating the phrase that seems to be for you today. As you think deeply on it, you might even memorize it. Committing biblical passages to memory allows us to hold them in our hearts all day long. If you keep a journal, you might write the passage there. Let those words sink deeply into your heart.

Then pray those words back to God in your heart. Those words may call up visual images, smells, sounds, and feelings. Pay attention to what God is giving you in those words. Then respond in faith to what those words say to your heart. What do they call you to be and to do? Our humble response might take the form of praise, thanksgiving, joy, confession, or even cries of pain.

The final step in this "holy reading" is contemplation of God. The words from God that we receive deeply in our hearts lead us to him. Through these words, we experience union with the all-powerful God of love. And that encounter does not leave us unchanged. Contemplation leads us to kingdom action based on the reading. To what does this reading lead?

What keeps reading the Bible this way from becoming merely our own desires read back into Scripture? How do we know it is God's voice we hear and not our own?

Consider two things. One is prayer. We are asking God to open our hearts, minds, and lives to him. We ask to hear his voice, not ours and not the voice of the world around us.

The second thing that keeps this from being an exercise in self-deception is to study the Bible in community. By praying over Scripture in a group, we hear God's word together. God speaks through the other members of our group. The wisdom he gives them keeps us from private, selfish, and unusual interpretations. They help us keep our own voices in check, as we desire to listen to God alone.

HOW TO USE THIS COMMENTARY

This commentary provides assistance in holy reading of the Bible. It gives structure to daily personal devotions, family meditation, small group Bible studies, and church classes.

DAILY DEVOTIONAL

Listening, meditation, prayer, contemplation—how does this commentary fit into this way of Bible study? Consider it as a conversation partner. We have taken a section of Scripture and then broken it down into four short daily readings. After listening, meditating, praying, and contemplating the passage for the day, use the questions suggested in the commentary to provoke deeper reflection. This provides a structure for a daily fifteen minute devotional four days a week. On the fifth day, read the entire passage, meditate, and then use the questions to reflect on the meaning of the whole. On day six, take our meditations on the passage as conversation with another who has prayed over the text.

If you want to begin daily Bible reading but need guidance, this provides a Monday-Saturday experience that prepares the heart for worship and praise on Sunday. This structure also results in a communal reading of Scripture, instead of a private reading. Even if you use this commentary alone, you are not reading privately. God is at work in you and in the conversation you have with another (the author of the commentary) who has sought to hear God through this particular passage of the Bible.

FAMILY BIBLE STUDY

This commentary can also provide an arrangement for family Bible study. Many Christian parents want to lead their children in daily study but don't know where to begin or how to structure their time. Using the six-day plan outlined above means the entire family can read, meditate, pray, and reflect on the shorter passages, using the questions provided. On day five, they can review the entire passage, and then on day six, read the meditations in the commentary to prompt reflection and discussion. God will bless our families beyond our imaginations through the prayerful study of his word.

WEEKLY GROUP STUDY

This commentary can also structure small group Bible study. Each member of the group should have meditated over the daily readings and questions for the five days preceding the group meeting, using the method outlined above. The day before the group meeting, each member should read and reflect on the meditations in the commentary on that passage. You then can meet once a week to hear God's word together. In that group meeting, the method of holy reading would look something like this:

Listening

1. Five minutes of silence.
2. Slow reading of the biblical passage for that week.
3. A minute of silent meditation on the passage.
4. Briefly share with the group the word or phrase that struck you.

Personal Message

5. A second reading of the same passage.
6. A minute of silence.
7. Where does this touch your life today?
8. Responses: I hear, I see, etc.

Life Response

9. Brief silence.

10. What does God want you to do today in light of this text?

Group Prayer

11. Have each member of the group pray aloud for the person on his or her left, asking God to bless the word he has given them.

The procedure suggested here can be used in churches or in neighborhood Bible studies. Church members would use the daily readings Monday-Friday in their daily devotionals. This commentary intentionally provides no readings on the sixth day, so that we can spend Saturdays as a time of rest, not rest from Bible study, but a time to let God's word quietly work its way deep into our hearts. Sunday during Bible school or in home meetings, the group would meet to experience the weekly readings together, using the group method described above. It might be that the sermon for each Sunday could be on the passage for that week.

There are churches that have used this structure to great advantage. Members come to the worship assembly prepared to hear a word from God in that particular text. Much of the background information that is sometimes needed in a sermon has already been given. Preaching can be much more focused on a particular teaching. We strongly urge churches try this type of congregational approach to the study of God's word. In the hallways of those churches who have embraced this type of study, the talk is not of the local football team or the weather, but of the shared experience of the Word of God for that week.

And that is the purpose of our personal and communal study, to hear the voice of God, our loving Father who wants us to love him in return. He deeply desires a personal relationship with us. Father, Son, and Spirit make a home inside us (see John 14:16-17, 23). Our loving God speaks to his children! But we must listen for his voice. That listening is not a matter of gritting our teeth and trying harder to hear. Instead, it is part of our entire life with God. That is what Bible study is all about.

Through daily personal prayer and meditation on God's word, and through a communal reading of Scripture, our most important conversation partner—the Holy Spirit—will do his mysterious and marvelous work. Among other things, the Spirit pours God's love into our hearts (Romans 5:5), bears witness to our spirits that we are God's children (Romans 8:16), intercedes for us with God (Romans 8:26), and enlightens us as to God's will (Ephesians 1:17).

So this is an invitation to personal daily Bible study, to praying the Scriptures, to sharing with fellow believers, to hearing the voice of God. God will bless us, our families, our churches, and his world if we take the time to be still, listen, and be obedience to his word.

EPHESIANS:

TRUE COMMUNITY IN JESUS CHRIST

THE SPIRITUALITY OF EPHESIANS

Arguments concerning authorship of this letter are left to the critical commentaries. There is an unbroken tradition that Paul wrote the letter and strong evidence to support this belief. More problematic is the indication that it was written "to the saints in Ephesus." The earliest manuscripts do not include this designation. Besides this, Paul spent three years ministering in Ephesus, but the language indicates Paul did not know his recipients personally. "To the saints in Ephesus" was likely added at a later date for reasons about which we can only speculate. It is most likely intended to be a general letter for all churches of Asia Minor. It is a powerful letter, reminding churches who they are and how they should live as witnesses to the living Lord. It is a call to be an authentic community built around the gift of life and forgiveness in Christ Jesus.

In Christ

Paul began the letter with a rousing reminder that all we have is because of and given through Christ. This theme permeates the entire epistle. By God's marvelous grace we have been made alive in Christ so that we might reign with him. One of our greatest needs in today's world is to recover the incredibly high calling we have been given in Christ! Paul chose to see his life of ministry as a gift of God's grace. Do we see the purpose of our existence in the same way? Read each segment of the text with a deep sense of gratitude for what you have "in Christ."

A Unified Church

Paul understood the importance of unity as a profound witness to the world of the power of the gospel. In Christ, all barriers have been removed. As significant as the Jewish/Gentile division was, it had been abolished by the peace established through the blood of Jesus. Paul's vision of the church presented in this letter—working together for the glory of God—is one of the most compelling in the entire Bible.

Living As Children Of Light

Because of the life we have received through the sacrifice of Jesus Christ, we must take our lives seriously. Non-believers have no reason to live a life for good. The Christian has the privilege and calling of demonstrating the superiority of a life filled with the light of God. Paul challenges us to imitate God in all our conduct. Only then will the non-believing world have a chance to repent and embrace the kingdom of God. For Paul, the key to faithful proclamation was faithfully living as children of light.

HOUSEHOLD CODE

To Paul, the family was tremendously important to the church. He provided specific instructions for godly interaction in families. While household codes (rules for family living) were not unusual in the ancient world, Paul's teachings were. They called for the husband/wife relationship to model the sacrificial relationship of Christ and his church. All familial and even slave relationships were to model the giving of one's self for the needs of another. While our world has changed much, our concern for one another within our families must reflect we are "in Christ."

Read slowly. Soak in the rich teachings of Paul that will lead us more deeply in life in Christ Jesus. Indeed, he is above all!

"Lord of lords, may your love for all be seen through your church as we accept the call to be dispensers of your grace. Through our Lord Jesus, Amen."

SPIRITUAL BLESSINGS IN JESUS
Christ (1:1-23)

DAY ONE READING AND QUESTIONS

[1] Paul, an apostle of Christ Jesus by the will of God,

To the saints in Ephesus, the faithful in Christ Jesus:

[2] Grace and peace to you from God our Father and the Lord Jesus Christ.

[3] Praise be to the God and Father of our Lord Jesus Christ, who has blessed us in the heavenly realms with every spiritual blessing in Christ.

1. Why do you think Paul began by identifying himself as an apostle?

2. How did Paul describe those to whom he was writing?

3. With what have we been blessed, according to Paul? Does this mean anything to you personally? Why or why not?

DAY TWO READING AND QUESTIONS

[4] For he chose us in him before the creation of the world to be holy and blameless in his sight. In love [5] he predestined us to be adopted as his sons through Jesus Christ, in accordance with his pleasure and will— [6] to the praise of his glorious grace, which he has freely given us in the One he loves. [7] In him we have redemption through his blood, the forgiveness of sins, in accordance with the riches of God's grace [8] that he lavished on us with all wisdom and understanding. [9] And he made

known to us the mystery of his will according to his good pleasure, which he purposed in Christ, [10] to be put into effect when the times will have reached their fulfillment—to bring all things in heaven and on earth together under one head, even Christ.

1. When were we chosen in Jesus Christ? Why is this significant?

2. How do we have forgiveness? What has been given to provide forgiveness for us?

3. What is the purpose of all that God has done and is doing? Why is this important to us?

DAY THREE READING AND QUESTIONS

[11] In him we were also chosen, having been predestined according to the plan of him who works out everything in conformity with the purpose of his will, [12] in order that we, who were the first to hope in Christ, might be for the praise of his glory. [13] And you also were included in Christ when you heard the word of truth, the gospel of your salvation. Having believed, you were marked in him with a seal, the promised Holy Spirit [14] who is a deposit guaranteeing our inheritance until the redemption of those who are God's possession—to the praise of his glory.

1. What does it mean to be or exist "for the praise of his glory?"

2. What is the seal that marks us as God's possession?

3. In what sense is our inheritance in Christ guaranteed?

DAY FOUR READING AND QUESTIONS

[15] For this reason, ever since I heard about your faith in the Lord Jesus and your love for all the saints, [16] I have not stopped giving thanks

for you, remembering you in my prayers. [17] I keep asking that the God of our Lord Jesus Christ, the glorious Father, may give you the Spirit of wisdom and revelation, so that you may know him better. [18] I pray also that the eyes of your heart may be enlightened in order that you may know the hope to which he has called you, the riches of his glorious inheritance in the saints, [19] and his incomparably great power for us who believe. That power is like the working of his mighty strength, [20] which he exerted in Christ when he raised him from the dead and seated him at his right hand in the heavenly realms, [21] far above all rule and authority, power and dominion, and every title that can be given, not only in the present age but also in the one to come. [22] And God placed all things under his feet and appointed him to be head over everything for the church, [23] which is his body, the fullness of him who fills everything in every way.

1. *Why did Paul give constant thanks for those to whom he was writing?*

2. *Why did Paul want his readers to have a spirit of wisdom and revelation?*

3. *What was Paul's view of the exalted Christ? Why is this important to us?*

DAY FIVE READING AND QUESTIONS

Reread the entire text (1:1-23)

1. *Do you see your life in the context of what God is doing in the world? Why or why not?*

2. *Does the redeeming work of Jesus for you affect your daily life? Do you often reflect on the gift of redemption through the blood of Jesus? Why or why not?*

3. Have the "eyes of your heart" been enlightened by the word of God? How so?

MEDITATION

If I could name one need for the Christian in today's world, it would be to recover (discover?) our identity in Christ Jesus. It is an invitation into a new reality, a different framing story. The world would have us define ourselves by what we have and what we do. Jesus invites us to live in the kingdom of God, where we have an identity based on who God is. If we accept this invitation, we become participants in a plan that predates the universe itself! We have been called to be a holy people— fully set apart for the purposes of God.

It is to this end that God sent Jesus Christ. So now, in him, we have everything we need! In him we have redemption, we have been given the mystery of God's will—we have been called to be a part of God's work to reconcile the world to himself! Our life has meaning; we have been given a purpose beyond anything this world could offer.

Paul desperately wanted his readers to understand the exalted nature of their calling. He was convinced that the better they knew the will of God for them, the more meaningful their lives would become. He wanted "the eyes of their hearts" to be enlightened so they might be confident about their purpose and their wonderful inheritance.

How does this reading strike you? How do you see your life? Are you seeking significance in a story other than God's? In Christ Jesus we have everything we need in abundance. However, life in Christ calls for our complete surrender to Jesus. We can't be in Jesus and of the world. For us to be what God intends, we must be set apart for his purposes. There is no other way to life.

"Creator God, thank you for giving us a purpose and identity long before we were born. May the eyes of our hearts be enlightened so that we may see the glory of your promises to us in Christ."

OUR LIFE IS JESUS
(2:1-22)

DAY ONE READING AND QUESTIONS

2:1 As for you, you were dead in your transgressions and sins, 2 in which you used to live when you followed the ways of this world and of the ruler of the kingdom of the air, the spirit who is now at work in those who are disobedient. 3 All of us also lived among them at one time, gratifying the cravings of our sinful nature and following its desires and thoughts. Like the rest, we were by nature objects of wrath. 4 But because of his great love for us, God, who is rich in mercy, 5 made us alive with Christ even when we were dead in transgressions—it is by grace you have been saved. 6 And God raised us up with Christ and seated us with him in the heavenly realms in Christ Jesus, 7 in order that in the coming ages he might show the incomparable riches of his grace, expressed in his kindness to us in Christ Jesus. 8 For it is by grace you have been saved, through faith—and this not from yourselves, it is the gift of God— 9 not by works, so that no one can boast. 10 For we are God's workmanship, created in Christ Jesus to do good works, which God prepared in advance for us to do.

1. Was there a time in your life when you felt dead in your sins? If so, take a moment to thank God for the forgiveness you have found through Jesus.

2. *Why is it important to acknowledge that it is the action of God who makes us alive with Christ and not something we have done to deserve his mercy?*

3. *According to Paul, what is it that saves us? Again, why is this important to acknowledge?*

DAY TWO READING AND QUESTIONS

[11] Therefore, remember that formerly you who are Gentiles by birth and called "uncircumcised" by those who call themselves "the circumcision" (that done in the body by the hands of men)— [12] remember that at that time you were separate from Christ, excluded from citizenship in Israel and foreigners to the covenants of the promise, without hope and without God in the world. [13] But now in Christ Jesus you who once were far away have been brought near through the blood of Christ.

1. *Why did Paul want the Gentiles to remember that they were once separate from Christ?*

2. *Because the Gentiles were not included in the covenants of the promise, what did they not have?*

3. *How were the Gentiles (which includes most of us) brought near to God?*

DAY THREE READING AND QUESTIONS

[14] For he himself is our peace, who has made the two one and has destroyed the barrier, the dividing wall of hostility, [15] by abolishing in his flesh the law with its commandments and regulations. His purpose was to create in himself one new man out of the two, thus making peace, [16] and in this one body to reconcile both of them to God through the cross, by which he put to death their hostility. [17] He came and preached

peace to you who were far away and peace to those who were near. [18] For through him we both have access to the Father by one Spirit.

1. *How was the dividing wall of hostility between the Jew and the Gentile destroyed?*

2. *How is it that out of two one man of peace was to be made? How do we participate in this peace?*

3. *What gives us access to the Father by one Spirit?*

DAY FOUR READING AND QUESTIONS

[19] Consequently, you are no longer foreigners and aliens, but fellow citizens with God's people and members of God's household, [20] built on the foundation of the apostles and prophets, with Christ Jesus himself as the chief cornerstone. [21] In him the whole building is joined together and rises to become a holy temple in the Lord. [22] And in him you too are being built together to become a dwelling in which God lives by his Spirit.

1. *What does it mean to be a fellow citizen with God's people and a member of God's household?*

2. *In what sense are we built on the foundation of the apostles and prophets, with Christ as the chief cornerstone?*

3. *Into what are we being built?*

DAY FIVE READING AND QUESTIONS

Reread the entire text (2:1-22)

1. *Do you regularly reflect on the free gift of life you have been given through Jesus? Why or why not?*

2. What do you think are the good works prepared before hand for you to do? (Be specific—these should be actions that come from your gifts and special abilities.)

3. Have you considered your noble calling to be an active, living part of the temple of God on this earth?

MEDITATION

There is no other story in the world that can compare to this. We were enemies of God, dead in our sins, living for all the wrong reasons, when God in his great mercy made us alive in and through Christ! He did this to demonstrate the incomparable richness of his grace to all ages, now and yet to come. We are living demonstrations of the grace of God. Once hopelessly lost in our sinful cravings, now we are free to live the life for which we were created—to do good works.

Does this describe you? Some are offended by Paul's words. After all, they were raised in Christian homes and have always gone to church. How could anyone suggest that they were at some point hopelessly lost sinners? Of course, they acknowledge they have been saved by Jesus—but saved from what? Unless we recognize our hopeless state without Jesus, we will never value appropriately the gift of God's grace. We will pay lip service to grace, but we will not likely surrender our lives to him in gratitude. As a result, we will continue to allow barriers to separate us from one another, to keep us from being God's united family. Why? Because we are depending on our being right instead of God making us righteous.

God's grace, when properly understood, tears down anything that divides believers. Why? Because we are given a new identity in Christ. We share a common story with all humanity. All desperately need the saving grace of God given through faith in Jesus Christ. Those who claim this gift are no longer foreigners and strangers, but are made are a part of God's household, becoming the very dwelling place of God in the world.

What an incredible story of love and rescue. Raised from the dead through Jesus, we can now be fully alive!

"Rescuing Lord, may we see clearly our desperate need for your rescue. Use us to proclaim your love and grace in such a way that others will want to join us in the only true story of life."

TO HIM WHO IS ABLE
(3:1-21)

DAY ONE READING AND QUESTIONS

3:1 For this reason I, Paul, the prisoner of Christ Jesus for the sake of you Gentiles—

2 Surely you have heard about the administration of God's grace that was given to me for you, 3 that is, the mystery made known to me by revelation, as I have already written briefly. 4 In reading this, then, you will be able to understand my insight into the mystery of Christ, 5 which was not made known to men in other generations as it has now been revealed by the Spirit to God's holy apostles and prophets. 6 This mystery is that through the gospel the Gentiles are heirs together with Israel, members together of one body, and sharers together in the promise in Christ Jesus.

1. How was Paul a prisoner of Christ Jesus for the sake of Gentiles?

2. How was Paul given the message that he preached?

3. What was the "mystery of Christ?"

DAY TWO READING AND QUESTIONS

7 I became a servant of this gospel by the gift of God's grace given me through the working of his power. 8 Although I am less than the least of all God's people, this grace was given me: to preach to the Gentiles the unsearchable riches of Christ, 9 and to make plain to everyone the

administration of this mystery, which for ages past was kept hidden in God, who created all things. [10] His intent was that now, through the church, the manifold wisdom of God should be made known to the rulers and authorities in the heavenly realms, [11] according to his eternal purpose which he accomplished in Christ Jesus our Lord. [12] In him and through faith in him we may approach God with freedom and confidence. [13] ask you, therefore, not to be discouraged because of my sufferings for you, which are your glory.

1. *Why is it significant that Paul viewed his ministry to the Gentiles as a gift of God's grace? (Remember who Paul was before his conversion).*

2. *What is God's design for his church according to these verses? Are we doing this through our churches? Why or why not?*

3. *In what sense were Paul's sufferings to be considered the Gentiles' "glory?"*

DAY THREE READING AND QUESTIONS

[14] For this reason I kneel before the Father, [15] from whom his whole family in heaven and on earth derives its name. [16] I pray that out of his glorious riches he may strengthen you with power through his Spirit in your inner being, [17] so that Christ may dwell in your hearts through faith. And I pray that you, being rooted and established in love, [18] may have power, together with all the saints, to grasp how wide and long and high and deep is the love of Christ, [19] and to know this love that surpasses knowledge— that you may be filled to the measure of all the fullness of God.

1. *For what reason did Paul kneel before the Father, according to these verses?*

2. What was Paul's prayer for those he wrote?

3. How can we "know" a love that surpasses "knowledge"? Have you experienced this love?

DAY FOUR READING AND QUESTIONS

[20] Now to him who is able to do immeasurably more than all we ask or imagine, according to his power that is at work within us, [21] to him be glory in the church and in Christ Jesus throughout all generations, for ever and ever! Amen.

1. Are there limits to what God can do for us and through us?

2. How do we access such limitless power, which Paul says is at work within us?

3. How does the church bring God glory?

DAY FIVE READING AND QUESTIONS

Reread the entire text (3:1-21)

1. How do you view the work to which God has called you? Do you see your work as an opportunity to live a kingdom focused life?

2. Do we, as God's church, reflect the manifold wisdom of God to all who see our lives? If not, what can be done to return the church to this God-given calling?

3. Do you dream about what God might do through you? Do you take your deepest desires to God and ask for him to go beyond anything you can imagine?

MEDITATION

I cannot imagine a more meaningful passage of Scripture. When Rebecca (my wife) and I first met, I had no intention of becoming a minister or missionary (which I would do sooner than I could imagine). One thing I understood, though, was the truth of Ephesians 3:20- 21. While church work held little appeal to me, I believed in the power of God in believers' lives. Rebecca was kind enough to cross stitch these verses for me. To this day, wherever we have worked in the world, those verses are over my desk. As I teach, one of the greatest gifts I can bestow on my students is to invite them to live under the power of this truth—God can do more with you than you could ever dream or even imagine!

This reading has the potential to transform each of us, if we choose to live in it. Paul describes his life of ministry as a gift of God's grace. Would Paul have ever chosen his God-given work? Do you think if there was a "University of Jerusalem" Paul would have considered majoring in "Mission to the Gentiles?" Are you kidding? He might have taken a course on "Keeping Oneself Pure from the Gentiles" or maybe "How to Live Separated from Gentiles." But something happened along the way. He encountered Jesus. Now, he was given what he chose to see as "a gift"—to explain the mystery of God to those he formerly despised—the Gentiles.

Paul wanted his readers to find what he had found—the joy of living a radical life of faith in the power of God to do things beyond one's dreams. The offer remains open. Do we choose to live in faith that God has us right where he wants us? This is our choice. The circumstances of our lives should not change this understanding of life. Even if we are in the middle of deep suffering, we can choose to embrace the view of life offered by Paul: God is at work through us right where we are. Are you living in his immeasurable power? If so, you will join Paul is his song of praise, "to him be the glory forever and ever. Amen."

"Sovereign Lord, teach us to see our lives, right where we are, as launching points for your ministry. Help us see your guiding hand so that we might follow your dreams for our lives. Forgive us when we are satisfied with less."

THE BODY OF CHRIST IN ACTION

(4:1–28)

DAY ONE READING AND QUESTIONS

[4:1] As a prisoner for the Lord, then, I urge you to live a life worthy of the calling you have received. [2] Be completely humble and gentle; be patient, bearing with one another in love. [3] Make every effort to keep the unity of the Spirit through the bond of peace. [4] There is one body and one Spirit—just as you were called to one hope when you were called—[5] one Lord, one faith, one baptism; [6] one God and Father of all, who is over all and through all and in all.

[7] But to each one of us grace has been given as Christ apportioned it. [8] This is why it says:

"When he ascended on high,
he led captives in his train
and gave gifts to men."

[9] (What does "he ascended" mean except that he also descended to the lower, earthly regions ? [10] He who descended is the very one who ascended higher than all the heavens, in order to fill the whole universe.)

1. *How does Paul describe a life worthy of God's calling? Does this describe your life?*

2. *From what does true unity come? What is our role is this unity?*

3. *What has each of us been given by Christ as he ascended victoriously into heaven?*

we are all ONE iN CHRIST

35

DAY TWO READING AND QUESTIONS

[11] It was he who gave some to be apostles, some to be prophets, some to be evangelists, and some to be pastors and teachers, [12] to prepare God's people for works of service, so that the body of Christ may be built up [13] until we all reach unity in the faith and in the knowledge of the Son of God and become mature, attaining to the whole measure of the fullness of Christ.

[14] Then we will no longer be infants, tossed back and forth by the waves, and blown here and there by every wind of teaching and by the cunning and craftiness of men in their deceitful scheming. [15] Instead, speaking the truth in love, we will in all things grow up into him who is the Head, that is, Christ. [16] From him the whole body, joined and held together by every supporting ligament, grows and builds itself up in love, as each part does its work.

1. *For what purpose was leadership given to the church? What is the role of leaders according to this passage?*

2. *What is the goal of the building up of the body of Christ? What are we to all reach and attain?*

3. *How does the church grow according to these verses?*

DAY THREE READING AND QUESTIONS

[17] So I tell you this, and insist on it in the Lord, that you must no longer live as the Gentiles do, in the futility of their thinking. [18] They are darkened in their understanding and separated from the life of God because of the ignorance that is in them due to the hardening of their hearts. [19] Having lost all sensitivity, they have given themselves over to sensuality so as to indulge in every kind of impurity, with a continual lust for more.

[20] You, however, did not come to know Christ that way. [21] Surely you heard of him and were taught in him in accordance with the truth that is

in Jesus. [22] You were taught, with regard to your former way of life, to put off your old self, which is being corrupted by its deceitful desires; [23] to be made new in the attitude of your minds; [24] and to put on the new self, created to be like God in true righteousness and holiness.

1. *How does one live "in the futility" of one's thinking? How is this kind of life demonstrated?*

2. *How does Paul describe a life "separated from God?" Have you seen this kind of life?*

3. *How does the truth in Jesus save us from such futile living? What must we intentionally do to receive the life Jesus offers?*

DAY FOUR READING AND QUESTIONS

[25] Therefore each of you must put off falsehood and speak truthfully to his neighbor, for we are all members of one body. [26] "In your anger do not sin" : Do not let the sun go down while you are still angry, [27] and do not give the devil a foothold. [28] He who has been stealing must steal no longer, but must work, doing something useful with his own hands, that he may have something to share with those in need.

1. *Why must we put off falsehood?*

2. *What is Paul's teaching concerning anger?*

3. *Why should a thief no longer steal? What should he do instead? Why?*

DAY FIVE READING AND QUESTIONS

Reread the entire text (4:1-28)

1. What should we do in order to live in unity with all of our brothers and sisters? Do you have unresolved conflicts with brothers and sisters in Christ? If so, seek to resolve them.

2. What is your gift? How might it contribute to the strength of the body of believers with whom you worship?

3. Do you intentionally and purposefully live as a "child of light?" Why or why not? What could you do to help your light shine more brightly? (Think of several specific things and take the time to pray about them on a regular basis).

MEDITATION

These verses contain the most complete picture of the church in action in all of the New Testament. Paul appeals to the church to maintain the unity of the Spirit, so that it can function as a well-developed, well-trained body. While there are many different gifts given to believers, they are given by one Lord for one purpose—to glorify God. It is for this reason that leaders are gifted or given to the church. Their role in God's plan is to equip all the different parts of the body so that they might function according to their God-given purpose of ministry. Each part (member) is to mature fully in the knowledge and image of Jesus Christ. The goal of church leaders, according to this passage, is to lead each member to live like Jesus in every circumstance of their lives. The translation of the passage, "speaking the truth in love" is a bit misleading (4:15). The verb "speaking" is not present in the Greek text. Paul used a verb that doesn't exist in the English language, so "speaking" has been inserted by the translators. The literal translation is "truthing it in love in all things." The call is more than to speak the truth in love. We are to live the truth in love in every action of our lives and every word that we speak.

If you are looking for a biblical pattern for church growth, this is it. When every member is fully matured in the knowledge and image of Christ, when all believers embody truth in all they do and say, when each contributes their gifts for the common good of the body (the church), the church will grow. According to Paul, numerical growth is not the goal of the church, but rather the consequence of a healthy body. If the church is healthy, maturing and ministering in the image of Christ, it will grow.

What is the goal of your life? What is the vision of the church of which you are a part? Are you growing toward the image of Jesus in everything you do? Have you put away the old life of darkness—living for self or for the world?

"Gracious Gift-giver, thank you for the new life you offer us. May we have the courage and the understanding to live according to your purposes. May your church function as you has designed. May we live the truth in love in all we do and say."

BE IMITATORS OF GOD

(4:29-5:20)

DAY ONE READING AND QUESTIONS

²⁹ Do not let any unwholesome talk come out of your mouths, but only what is helpful for building others up according to their needs, that it may benefit those who listen. ³⁰ And do not grieve the Holy Spirit of God, with whom you were sealed for the day of redemption. ³¹ Get rid of all bitterness, rage and anger, brawling and slander, along with every form of malice. ³² Be kind and compassionate to one another, forgiving each other, just as in Christ God forgave you.

⁵:¹ Be imitators of God, therefore, as dearly loved children ² and live a life of love, just as Christ loved us and gave himself up for us as a fragrant offering and sacrifice to God.

1. For what purpose should we speak, according to Paul?

2. How do we grieve the Holy Spirit?

3. Why should we be an imitator of God? How does Paul describe such a life?

DAY TWO READING AND QUESTIONS

³ But among you there must not be even a hint of sexual immorality, or of any kind of impurity, or of greed, because these are improper for God's holy people. ⁴ Nor should there be obscenity, foolish talk or coarse

joking, which are out of place, but rather thanksgiving. [5] For of this you can be sure: No immoral, impure or greedy person—such a man is an idolater—has any inheritance in the kingdom of Christ and of God. [6] Let no one deceive you with empty words, for because of such things God's wrath comes on those who are disobedient. [7] Therefore do not be partners with them.

1. *What is improper behavior for God's holy people according to this passage?*

2. *What should be spoken in the place of improper words?*

3. *Is God's wrath something you fear? Why or why not? Why does Paul refer to God's wrath?*

DAY THREE READING AND QUESTIONS

[8] For you were once darkness, but now you are light in the Lord. Live as children of light [9] (for the fruit of the light consists in all goodness, righteousness and truth) [10] and find out what pleases the Lord. [11] Have nothing to do with the fruitless deeds of darkness, but rather expose them. [12] For it is shameful even to mention what the disobedient do in secret. [13] But everything exposed by the light becomes visible, [14] for it is light that makes everything visible. This is why it is said:

"Wake up, O sleeper,
　　rise from the dead,
　and Christ will shine on you."

1. *What does it mean to live as children of light?*

2. *How are fruitless deeds of darkness exposed by children of light?*

3. *Some have suggested verse 14 quotes a baptismal poem or song. Why would Paul refer to this at this point in his letter?*

DAY FOUR READING AND QUESTIONS

[15] Be very careful, then, how you live—not as unwise but as wise, [16] making the most of every opportunity, because the days are evil. [17] Therefore do not be foolish, but understand what the Lord's will is. [18] Do not get drunk on wine, which leads to debauchery. Instead, be filled with the Spirit. [19] Speak to one another with psalms, hymns and spiritual songs. Sing and make music in your heart to the Lord, [20] always giving thanks to God the Father for everything, in the name of our Lord Jesus Christ.

1. *What do you think Paul meant when he said "the days are evil?"*

2. *How are we to be "filled with the Spirit?" What behavior does such a filling cause?*

3. *For what should we give thanks? Do you do this? Why or why not?*

DAY FIVE READING AND QUESTIONS

Reread the entire text (4:29-5:20)

1. *Try getting through an entire day speaking only words which build others up, according to their needs. Do you find this easy or difficult? Why?*

2. *Do you consider yourself a "child of light?" If not, why not? If so, how does this identity influence your daily life?*

3. *How can we encourage one another to understand the value of each day in our lives?*

MEDITATION

Once again, Paul challenges us with the all-encompassing nature of authentic faith in Jesus. We are to consider the purpose of every word we speak. Is it to build up or tear down? Paul doesn't tell us what to say, but he does tell us what should be the motivation for all we say. The life to which we are called is one of gracious service, and this must permeate our every word and action. Kindness and a forgiving spirit should be evident in all our interactions with all people. Why? Because this is exactly what Jesus did for us. In living this way his life was a fragrant aroma, pleasing to God. We are invited to be that same aroma.

My father was a wonderful man. I loved him dearly. One of the things I enjoyed most was bringing him joy through what I did. I really wanted to please him. The day before he died I sat at his bedside and we reminisced together. Towards the end of our conversation, he smiled and blessed me richly with these words, "I am proud to call you my son. You have been a joy to me." He closed his eyes and smiled, remembering our lives together. He chose not to think about all the trouble and heartache I had caused (I was a terror as a child—ask my siblings). His memory of me at that moment was lovingly subjective and wonderfully forgiving! But I will never forget that moment. In spite of all my sins, I brought joy to my father!

What do you do when you encounter an aroma that is particularly pleasing? I stop and close my eyes. I close my mouth and take a deep breath through my nose. It is a delightful experience. Many times the aroma is associated with a particularly pleasant memory. It calls for joyful remembrance and contemplation. Can you imagine gifting God with such a sensation? This is the life to which we are invited. Living as children of light, as imitators of God, is both a privilege and an intentional discipline. It calls us to purposely pursue a life of goodness and righteousness as modeled by Christ Jesus. It also calls us to shun behaviors and speech patterns which do not honor God. When we live as Jesus lived we bring a joyful remembrance to the Father of light. Imagine God closing his eyes, inhaling deeply through his nose, remembering the sweet aroma of Jesus—all because we choose to honor him with our words and actions.

"Loving Father, with all that is in us, we want to cause you to smile. We cannot fully know how much you love us, but we know you do because of all you have given. May our lives be a sweet aroma of praise to you."

PUT ON THE FULL ARMOR OF GOD

(5:21-6:24)

DAY ONE READING AND QUESTIONS

[21] Submit to one another out of reverence for Christ.

[22] Wives, submit to your husbands as to the Lord. [23] For the husband is the head of the wife as Christ is the head of the church, his body, of which he is the Savior. [24] Now as the church submits to Christ, so also wives should submit to their husbands in everything.

[25] Husbands, love your wives, just as Christ loved the church and gave himself up for her [26] to make her holy, cleansing her by the washing with water through the word, [27] and to present her to himself as a radiant church, without stain or wrinkle or any other blemish, but holy and blameless. [28] In this same way, husbands ought to love their wives as their own bodies. He who loves his wife loves himself. [29] After all, no one ever hated his own body, but he feeds and cares for it, just as Christ does the church— [30] for we are members of his body. [31] "For this reason a man will leave his father and mother and be united to his wife, and the two will become one flesh." [32] This is a profound mystery—but I am talking about Christ and the church. [33] However, each one of you also must love his wife as he loves himself, and the wife must respect her husband.

1. *Why is it important to recognize that Paul begins this section with the command to submit to one another out of reverence to Christ? How does this affect how we read the rest of the passage?*

2. *How does the church submit to Christ? How would a wife submit to her husband in the same way?*

3. In what way is the husband to love his wife? Give examples of how this would look in a married couple's day to day life.

DAY TWO READING AND QUESTIONS

⁶:¹ Children, obey your parents in the Lord, for this is right. ² "Honor your father and mother"—which is the first commandment with a promise— ³ "that it may go well with you and that you may enjoy long life on the earth."

⁴ Fathers, do not exasperate your children; instead, bring them up in the training and instruction of the Lord.

⁵ Slaves, obey your earthly masters with respect and fear, and with sincerity of heart, just as you would obey Christ. ⁶ Obey them not only to win their favor when their eye is on you, but like slaves of Christ, doing the will of God from your heart. ⁷ Serve wholeheartedly, as if you were serving the Lord, not men, ⁸ because you know that the Lord will reward everyone for whatever good he does, whether he is slave or free.

⁹ And masters, treat your slaves in the same way. Do not threaten them, since you know that he who is both their Master and yours is in heaven, and there is no favoritism with him.

1. What is the promise for obedient children?

2. How are fathers to treat their children?

3. How were believing slaves and masters called to live? Why did Paul not speak out against slavery?

DAY THREE READING AND QUESTIONS

¹⁰ Finally, be strong in the Lord and in his mighty power. ¹¹ Put on the full armor of God so that you can take your stand against the devil's schemes. ¹² For our struggle is not against flesh and blood, but

against the rulers, against the authorities, against the powers of this dark world and against the spiritual forces of evil in the heavenly realms. [13] Therefore put on the full armor of God, so that when the day of evil comes, you may be able to stand your ground, and after you have done everything, to stand. [14] Stand firm then, with the belt of truth buckled around your waist, with the breastplate of righteousness in place, [15] and with your feet fitted with the readiness that comes from the gospel of peace. [16] In addition to all this, take up the shield of faith, with which you can extinguish all the flaming arrows of the evil one. [17] Take the helmet of salvation and the sword of the Spirit, which is the word of God. [18] And pray in the Spirit on all occasions with all kinds of prayers and requests. With this in mind, be alert and always keep on praying for all the saints.

1. Why do we need the armor of God? Who is the one who would destroy us? Do you fear the attacks of Satan? Why or why not?

2. What are the pieces of armor provided by God? Why do you think Paul uses this metaphor for how the Christian should be prepared?

3. How does Paul tell us to pray? How do we apply this to our daily lives?

DAY FOUR READING AND QUESTIONS

[19] Pray also for me, that whenever I open my mouth, words may be given me so that I will fearlessly make known the mystery of the gospel, [20] for which I am an ambassador in chains. Pray that I may declare it fearlessly, as I should.

[21] Tychicus, the dear brother and faithful servant in the Lord, will tell you everything, so that you also may know how I am and what I am doing. [22] I am sending him to you for this very purpose, that you may know how we are, and that he may encourage you.

[23] Peace to the brothers, and love with faith from God the Father and the Lord Jesus Christ. [24] Grace to all who love our Lord Jesus Christ with an undying love.

1. For what did Paul ask the believers to pray on his behalf? What does this tell us about Paul?

2. What was Tychicus to do?

3. What do you think Paul meant by "love with faith?"

DAY FIVE READING AND QUESTIONS

Reread the entire text (5:21-6:24)

1. Do you intentionally practice the discipline of submission? Do you find it difficult to submit to the will of another? Why?

2. Do your personal relationships bear the image of Christ? Do you love others with Christ's self-giving love?

3. Do you see yourself in the context of a battle with Satan? Do you intentionally prepare yourself for battle on a daily basis? How might you "put on the armor of God" in a deliberate way?

MEDITATION

What is appropriate behavior for the Christian in today's world? How do we demonstrate that we are children of light in our everyday relationships? Paul calls us to submit to one another out of reverence for Christ. He then proceeds to explain how that works out for spouses, children, slaves, and masters. His intent was not to approve or disapprove of the roles—these were simply the most common relationships represented in the early church. While we might wish that Paul had described more egalitarian roles in marriage, and we would certainly wish that Paul would have expressed disdain for slavery—this misses the point of what he was teaching. If we are to be imitators of God, this is to be done faithfully right where we are. Today, it seems our main concern in relationships is "what's in it for me?" Paul's main concern was, "How do I honor God in my present situation in life?"

It is for this reason Paul instructs wives to express the image of God through loving submission to their husbands. Husbands are to express that divine image through giving themselves to their wives with a love that mirrors the life-giving sacrifice of Jesus. Together, the Christian couple demonstrates to the world the mystery of two becoming one. Children are to obey their parents; parents are to train their children in the teachings of the Lord. Slaves are called to be obedient to their masters as if their masters where Jesus Christ, serving them wholeheartedly. Masters are to treat their slaves in the same way. With the exception of instructions to parents/children, these would have been considered radical teachings! Authentic life is not about personal rights and individual freedom, it is about expressing the image of God through whatever situation in which you find yourself—good or bad. So, here is the challenge for each of us. Do we reflect the image of God in our marriage relationships? Do we reflect the image of God as parents/children? How about in our place of employment? What, or who, do people see in us?

There is one who would destroy the image of God in us. We need to be strong and prepared to stand against Satan's attacks. Paul compares our preparation against evil to a warrior dressing for battle. God supplies our every need to not only protect ourselves, but to attack the evil one and his work. But we have to decide to put the armor on. We have to pick up the sword. If we are committed to demonstrating to the world what it means to be a child of light and an imitator of God himself, we are engaged in a mighty battle. Develop the daily discipline of putting on the armor of God!

"Almighty God, thank you for the privilege of serving you. May we reflect on each of our roles in life and consider what you would have us be to your glory. Free us from self-will. Arm us for the battle. May we glorify you in our every relationship, every word, and every action."

PHILIPPIANS:

JESUS CHRIST, THE SONG OF LIFE

THE SPIRITUALITY OF PHILIPPIANS

Of all of Paul's letters, Philippians is the most joyful. While Paul had concerns to address, for the most part his epistle was an expression of gratitude and hope. We know of the founding of the church in Philippi through Luke's account in Acts 16. Paul and his party initially met Lydia on the riverside, were invited to stay with her, healed a slave girl of a demonic spirit which resulted in their being thrown into prison. After being freed by an earthquake, they were able to convert the jailor under whose care they were placed. It is a joy to see what that church had become. The occasion for this writing was the church in Philippi sending another financial gift to Paul—this letter is Paul's response for that gift. Consider the following themes:

THANKSGIVING

Paul wanted to express his deep gratitude to God for the partnership of the church in Philippi. At the end of the letter he also expressed his thanksgiving for the gift sent to him, but not for the reasons we might expect (see the meditation for chapter four). Paul's greatest expression of gratitude, however, is to God for the life of ministry with which he has been blessed. If he dies, then he is with Jesus—praise God! If he lives, he ministers to his brothers and sisters in the Lord and proclaims the gospel to the lost—praise God! This letter helps us realize what a blessing we have in living in Christ Jesus our Lord!

REJOICE!

This is a letter of joy! True joy comes through reflecting on the many blessings we have in the Lord. Paul was joyful for his association with the Philippians, joyful because of his calling, joyful for what God was doing through the Philippians, joyful for what God was doing even through Paul's enemies—as long as they were preaching the Gospel! Paul was joyful for true friends like Timothy and Epaphroditus, joyful for his discovery of the value of knowing Jesus Christ, joyful in his anticipation of the Lord's return. So, what might his message be to us? "Rejoice in the Lord always. Let me say it again, rejoice" (4:4). This letter challenges us to be joyful in all circumstances of life.

AUTHENTIC TRANSFORMATION

Philippians 3 is one of the greatest texts in the Bible concerning authentic spiritual formation. Paul's description of giving up what was once of great value to him because of the surpassing value he found in knowing Christ Jesus is deeply challenging and wonderfully compelling. Paul's letter calls us to answer the difficult question, "What do we value and pursue most with our lives?" The truth is, if we are pursuing anything other than Jesus we are living for too little.

THE CHRIST HYMN

Is there any passage of greater beauty and value than the Christ hymn of 2:5-11? I attended a conference where a speaker convincingly proposed this passage as the main interpretive text for our lives. Do we have the attitude of Jesus? Are we being shaped by the story of the life of Jesus? Are we following him as a willing servant—one who would give up everything, even our lives—in order to glorify God?

Philippians is a feast for those interested in spiritual formation. Read it slowly, read it often. Read it, meditate on it, savor it and allow the Spirit to do his work!

"Loving Father, thank you for the joyous life you give us in Christ Jesus. May our lives be a source of joy for you. Through your Son, the reason for our joy, amen."

TO LIVE IS CHRIST, TO DIE IS GAIN

(1:1-30)

DAY ONE READING AND QUESTIONS

[1] Paul and Timothy, servants of Christ Jesus,

To all the saints in Christ Jesus at Philippi, together with the overseers and deacons:

[2] Grace and peace to you from God our Father and the Lord Jesus Christ.

[3] I thank my God every time I remember you. [4] In all my prayers for all of you, I always pray with joy [5] because of your partnership in the gospel from the first day until now, [6] being confident of this, that he who began a good work in you will carry it on to completion until the day of Christ Jesus.

[7] It is right for me to feel this way about all of you, since I have you in my heart; for whether I am in chains or defending and confirming the gospel, all of you share in God's grace with me. [8] God can testify how I long for all of you with the affection of Christ Jesus.

[9] And this is my prayer: that your love may abound more and more in knowledge and depth of insight, [10] so that you may be able to discern what is best and may be pure and blameless until the day of Christ, [11] filled with the fruit of righteousness that comes through Jesus Christ—to the glory and praise of God.

1. What was the reason for Paul's gratitude for the Philippians?

2. Of what was Paul confident? What did he mean by this?

3. What was Paul's prayer for the Philippians? Why?

DAY TWO READING AND QUESTIONS

[12] Now I want you to know, brothers, that what has happened to me has really served to advance the gospel. [13] As a result, it has become clear throughout the whole palace guard and to everyone else that I am in chains for Christ. [14] Because of my chains, most of the brothers in the Lord have been encouraged to speak the word of God more courageously and fearlessly.

[15] It is true that some preach Christ out of envy and rivalry, but others out of goodwill. [16] The latter do so in love, knowing that I am put here for the defense of the gospel. [17] The former preach Christ out of selfish ambition, not sincerely, supposing that they can stir up trouble for me while I am in chains. [18] But what does it matter? The important thing is that in every way, whether from false motives or true, Christ is preached. And because of this I rejoice.

1. How did Paul react to his imprisonment?

2. What happened as a result of Paul's imprisonment?

3. What was Paul's attitude toward those who were trying to cause him trouble while in prison? What does this tell us about Paul?

DAY THREE READINGS AND QUESTIONS

Yes, and I will continue to rejoice, [19] for I know that through your prayers and the help given by the Spirit of Jesus Christ, what has happened to me will turn out for my deliverance. [20] I eagerly expect and hope that I will in no way be ashamed, but will have sufficient courage so that now as always Christ will be exalted in my body, whether by life or by death. [21] For to me, to live is Christ and to die is gain. [22] If I am to go on living in the body, this will mean fruitful labor for me. Yet what shall I choose? I do not know! [23] I am torn between the two: I desire to depart and be with Christ, which is better by far; [24] but it is more necessary for you that I remain in the body. [25] Convinced of this, I know that I will remain, and I will continue with all of you for your progress and joy in the faith, [26] so that through my being with you again your joy in Christ Jesus will overflow on account of me.

1. *What do you think Paul means by "my deliverance?"*

2. *What do you think Paul means by saying "to live is Christ?" What would it look like to live this way?*

3. *How is it that Paul desired to depart, yet "chose" to stay? How do you view death?*

DAY FOUR READING AND QUESTIONS

[27] Whatever happens, conduct yourselves in a manner worthy of the gospel of Christ. Then, whether I come and see you or only hear about you in my absence, I will know that you stand firm in one spirit, contending as one man for the faith of the gospel [28] without being frightened in any way by those who oppose you. This is a sign to them that they will be destroyed, but that you will be saved—and that by God. [29] For it has been granted to you on behalf of Christ not only to believe on him, but also to suffer for him, [30] since you are going through the same struggle you saw I had, and now hear that I still have.

1. *What does Paul mean by encouraging his readers to "conduct yourselves in a manner worthy of the gospel of Christ?" How would that look?*

2. *Why should the Philippians not be afraid of those who might oppose them?*

3. How is it that it is granted to us not only to believe but also to suffer? How do you view personal suffering?

DAY FIVE READING AND QUESTIONS

Reread the entire text (1:1-1:20)

1. If Paul were to tell you that Christ would bring to completion the good work begun in you, what would that good work be? How can you make yourself more available to God and his work in you?

2. Have you ever had anyone do something to intentionally harm or disparage you? How did you react? What might you have done that would more fully honor God?

3. Can you say, "For me to live is Christ, and to die gain?" How might we help each other live in this way?

MEDITATION

Paul has much to teach us about how we view our own lives. Paul wants every believer to be full of joy and gratitude—no matter what the circumstances. With us living in a culture that floods our minds with the idea that life is good only when it is exactly as we want it—Paul's call to joy and thanksgiving in all circumstances is a real challenge!

Here is the question Paul asks throughout this letter of encouragement, "Where do you live? What is your address?" He is not asking about your physical home, he is asking about your heart. You either live in God's story of life or you don't. If you choose to live where God truly reigns, then bask in the sunshine of God's loving care. Reflect carefully on Paul's prayer for the Philippians. He wanted their love to abound and understanding to increase, so that they would more fully participate in the glorious righteousness of Christ until his return.

Paul wasn't just being optimistic. He was living fully in the kingdom of God. Even though he was imprisoned, being mistreated by fellow believers, even though he might soon be executed –all he could do was praise God and be filled with gratitude for his life. "For me to live is Christ, to die is gain." What a statement! There is no downside in this story of life. If you chose to live where God reigns, in the heart of his kingdom, your life in this world never loses meaning. And if you lose your life, you will find yourself with Christ Jesus in the presence of God for eternity!

For this reason, Paul challenges all of us, "Whatever happens, conduct yourselves in a manner worthy of the good news of Christ." If that means we are called to suffer, so be it. No one or no thing can take away the blessings and promises we have in Jesus Christ. That is, if you choose to live in that place where God reigns supreme!

"Sovereign God, Almighty King, teach us to live in that place where life is always meaningful and death itself is gain!"

THE CHRIST HYMN

(2:1-30)

DAY ONE READING AND QUESTIONS

²:¹ If you have any encouragement from being united with Christ, if any comfort from his love, if any fellowship with the Spirit, if any tenderness and compassion, ² then make my joy complete by being like-minded, having the same love, being one in spirit and purpose. ³ Do nothing out of selfish ambition or vain conceit, but in humility consider others better than yourselves. ⁴ Each of you should look not only to your own interests, but also to the interests of others.

1. How do you think the Philippian church answered this series of questions? Why? How would you answer his questions?

2. How could Paul's joy be made complete? Would he be joyful if he knew of the relationships in the family of faith of which you are a part?

3. How is it that we are to consider one another as better than ourselves? What would happen if an entire community of faith chose to see each other in this way?

DAY TWO READING AND QUESTIONS

⁵ Your attitude should be the same as that of Christ Jesus:
⁶ Who, being in very nature God,

did not consider equality with God something to be grasped,
[7] but made himself nothing,
taking the very nature of a servant,
being made in human likeness.
[8] And being found in appearance as a man,
he humbled himself and became obedient to death—
even death on a cross!
[9] Therefore God exalted him to the highest place
and gave him the name that is above every name,
[10] that at the name of Jesus every knee should bow,
in heaven and on earth and under the earth,
[11] and every tongue confess that Jesus Christ is Lord,
to the glory of God the Father.

1. In what way should our attitude be like that of Christ Jesus?

2. Why did Jesus not grasp his "equality with God?"

3. What was the result of Christ Jesus' obedient life, suffering, and death?

DAY THREE READING AND QUESTIONS

[12] Therefore, my dear friends, as you have always obeyed—not only in my presence, but now much more in my absence—continue to work out your salvation with fear and trembling, [13] for it is God who works in you to will and to act according to his good purpose.

[14] Do everything without complaining or arguing, [15] so that you may become blameless and pure, children of God without fault in a crooked and depraved generation, in which you shine like stars in the universe [16] as you hold out the word of life—in order that I may boast on the day of Christ that I did not run or labor for nothing. [17] But even if I am being poured out like a drink offering on the sacrifice and service coming from

your faith, I am glad and rejoice with all of you. [18] So you too should be glad and rejoice with me.

1. *How are we to work out our salvation if we are saved by God's grace?*

2. *Is this an overstatement, or did Paul really mean we are to do everything without complaining or arguing?*

3. *What do you think Paul meant by the believers shining like stars in the universe?*

DAY FOUR READING AND QUESTIONS

[19] I hope in the Lord Jesus to send Timothy to you soon, that I also may be cheered when I receive news about you. [20] I have no one else like him, who takes a genuine interest in your welfare. [21] For everyone looks out for his own interests, not those of Jesus Christ. [22] But you know that Timothy has proved himself, because as a son with his father he has served with me in the work of the gospel. [23] I hope, therefore, to send him as soon as I see how things go with me. [24] And I am confident in the Lord that I myself will come soon.

[25] But I think it is necessary to send back to you Epaphroditus, my brother, fellow worker and fellow soldier, who is also your messenger, whom you sent to take care of my needs. [26] For he longs for all of you and is distressed because you heard he was ill. [27] Indeed he was ill, and almost died. But God had mercy on him, and not on him only but also on me, to spare me sorrow upon sorrow. [28] Therefore I am all the more eager to send him, so that when you see him again you may be glad and I may have less anxiety. [29] Welcome him in the Lord with great joy, and honor men like him, [30] because he almost died for the work of Christ, risking his life to make up for the help you could not give me.

1. What made Timothy unique for Paul?

2. What image does Paul use to describe his relationship with Timothy? Do you have relationships in the Lord similar to this? A spiritual father or child? If so, take a moment to thank God for such a gift.

3. What does Paul ask the Philippians to do in receiving Epaphroditus? Why?

DAY FIVE READING AND QUESTIONS

Reread the entire text (2:1-30)

1. How would it change our churches if members did nothing out of self interest? Is this possible?

2. How can we encourage one another to embrace the story of life Jesus came to give us? Is the life of Jesus the model of life you pursue? Why or why not?

3. How is it that God works in us, to will and to act according to his purposes? How might we be more cooperative with God in this endeavor?

MEDITATION

This is the heart of the gospel. For all we have received in Jesus Christ, it means nothing unless our only intent in life is to be like him. Jesus came to save us not only from our sins but from ourselves. His pattern of life is unlike any other. Being God himself, he demonstrated life in its only true form—that of a servant fully submitted to God. The result of such a life? Exaltation to the highest place!

I can't help but think of the failure of the children of Israel. God called them to be a nation above all nations. They wanted that, but they insisted on doing it their own way. The results were tragic. We risk the same mistake. We all seek to be exalted. And so we should. We are the image of God—created for greatness! Yet, if we seek to exalt ourselves, we are as foolish as the child attempting to pick himself up by his own shoe-strings. The way up is down, and Jesus proved this by his amazing life.

So what will you do with your life? Will you be a star shining in the sky to God's glory? That is God's invitation. But there is only one way to get there. "If you would be my follower, deny yourself, pick up your cross daily, and follow me." We know these words. But will we sing the Christ hymn? "Your attitude should be the same as that of Christ Jesus: . . ." I challenge you to read these verses (2:6-11) and meditate on them every day. Let's make this song the theme of our lives.

"Dear Father, there are no words that can adequately express our amazement at what Jesus Christ was willing to do in order to show us the way to abundant life. Train our hearts and minds to sing our Savior's song of life. May we fully submit our lives to you after the example of our Lord."

SPIRITUAL TRANSFORMATION

(3:1-4:1)

DAY ONE READING AND QUESTIONS

^{3:1} Finally, my brothers, rejoice in the Lord! It is no trouble for me to write the same things to you again, and it is a safeguard for you.

² Watch out for those dogs, those men who do evil, those mutilators of the flesh. ³ For it is we who are the circumcision, we who worship by the Spirit of God, who glory in Christ Jesus, and who put no confidence in the flesh— ⁴ though I myself have reasons for such confidence.

If anyone else thinks he has reasons to put confidence in the flesh, I have more: ⁵ circumcised on the eighth day, of the people of Israel, of the tribe of Benjamin, a Hebrew of Hebrews; in regard to the law, a Pharisee; ⁶ as for zeal, persecuting the church; as for legalistic righteousness, faultless.

1. Who are the "mutilators of the flesh" of which Paul warns?

2. What are the marks of "true circumcision?" Do we bear these signs of authentic faith?

3. Did Paul have any reason to be proud of his earthly accomplishments? Why did Paul bring this up?

DAY TWO READING AND QUESTIONS

[7] But whatever was to my profit I now consider loss for the sake of Christ. [8] What is more, I consider everything a loss compared to the surpassing greatness of knowing Christ Jesus my Lord, for whose sake I have lost all things. I consider them rubbish, that I may gain Christ [9] and be found in him, not having a righteousness of my own that comes from the law, but that which is through faith in Christ—the righteousness that comes from God and is by faith. [10] I want to know Christ and the power of his resurrection and the fellowship of sharing in his sufferings, becoming like him in his death, [11] and so, somehow, to attain to the resurrection from the dead.

1. What did Paul find that was of greater value than earthly wealth and accomplishments?

2. What righteousness did Paul find? What does this mean?

3. What did Paul still want to know more about?

DAY THREE READING AND QUESTIONS

[12] Not that I have already obtained all this, or have already been made perfect, but I press on to take hold of that for which Christ Jesus took hold of me. [13] Brothers, I do not consider myself yet to have taken hold of it. But one thing I do: Forgetting what is behind and straining toward what is ahead, [14] I press on toward the goal to win the prize for which God has called me heavenward in Christ Jesus.

[15] All of us who are mature should take such a view of things. And if on some point you think differently, that too God will make clear to you. [16] Only let us live up to what we have already attained.

1. What had Paul not attained?

2. What did Paul choose to forget and what did Paul choose to pursue?

3. What is "the prize" of which Paul speaks?

DAY FOUR READING AND QUESTIONS

[17] Join with others in following my example, brothers, and take note of those who live according to the pattern we gave you. [18] For, as I have often told you before and now say again even with tears, many live as enemies of the cross of Christ. [19] Their destiny is destruction, their god is their stomach, and their glory is in their shame. Their mind is on earthly things. [20] But our citizenship is in heaven. And we eagerly await a Savior from there, the Lord Jesus Christ, [21] who, by the power that enables him to bring everything under his control, will transform our lowly bodies so that they will be like his glorious body.

[4:1] Therefore, my brothers, you whom I love and long for, my joy and crown, that is how you should stand firm in the Lord, dear friends!

1. What is the example Paul called his readers to follow? What are the specifics of such an example?

2. How does Paul describe the lives of those who are living as "enemies of the cross of Christ?"

3. What are the implications of our citizenship being in heaven?

DAY FIVE READING AND QUESTIONS

Reread the entire text (3:1-4:1)

1. What do you value most in your life? If it is not Jesus Christ as the model of life, why not? What can we do to help one another set the life and teachings of Jesus as the ultimate pursuit of our lives?

2. *What things that you once highly valued have become less attractive and meaningful to you? Why?*

3. *Paul said if our minds are on earthly things we are living as enemies of the cross. How could he say this? How can we encourage one another to live for things of true value?*

MEDITATION

This is one of my favorite texts in the Bible. For purposes of teaching personal spiritual formation, there simply is no more helpful passage. We see what Paul experienced when he encountered Jesus Christ and continued to grow in that relationship. Apparently his detractors accused him of teaching a gospel of emptying one's self because he had nothing of which to be proud. On the contrary—he had every reason to have pride in his material possessions and his earthy accomplishments. He simply saw how little value they had in comparison to knowing Christ Jesus.

Paul chose not to pursue earthly things because he saw them for what they were—meaningless when compared to something of far greater value. This, I think, is the key to allowing the Holy Spirit to transform us into the image of Jesus. When we see Jesus Christ for who he truly is, everything else we might pursue becomes disgusting trash. If there is anything we want more in life than to be like Jesus, we have yet to see him as truly is.

In today's world, this is a great challenge. We have heroes and heroines who have won our admiration yet they've done nothing of lasting value. We need to exalt Jesus so that our children and all others who know us see him clearly as the true hero of life. How do we do this? Study, prayer, and meditation—we need to intentionally deepen our understanding of who he is. In a world full of idols, we need to focus our hearts on Jesus until he becomes the only pursuit of our lives. Until then, we are simply satisfied with too little.

Paul tells us that an enemy of the cross is one whose mind is on earthly things. Why? Because he or she has not yet seen what Jesus offers in the place of earthly things. The power of the cross frees us from the pursuit of the meaningless so that we can, with Paul, forget what lies behind and pursue the righteousness that comes through a faith relationship with Jesus.

"Loving God, give us eyes to see our Lord in such a way that the pursuit of anything else would seem foolish."

REJOICE IN THE LORD

(4:2-23)

DAY ONE READING AND QUESTIONS

2 I plead with Euodia and I plead with Syntyche to agree with each other in the Lord. 3 Yes, and I ask you, loyal yokefellow, help these women who have contended at my side in the cause of the gospel, along with Clement and the rest of my fellow workers, whose names are in the book of life.

4 Rejoice in the Lord always. I will say it again: Rejoice! 5 Let your gentleness be evident to all. The Lord is near. 6 Do not be anxious about anything, but in everything, by prayer and petition, with thanksgiving, present your requests to God. 7 And the peace of God, which transcends all understanding, will guard your hearts and your minds in Christ Jesus.

1. What do we know of Euodia and Syntyche through these verses?

2. Why should we "rejoice always in the Lord"? Is this really possible?

3. What should replace worry in our lives, according to Paul?

DAY TWO READING AND QUESTIONS

8 Finally, brothers, whatever is true, whatever is noble, whatever is right, whatever is pure, whatever is lovely, whatever is admirable— if anything is excellent or praiseworthy—think about such things.

⁹ Whatever you have learned or received or heard from me, or seen in me—put it into practice. And the God of peace will be with you.

1. Why does Paul care about the things which occupy our thoughts?

2. List things in your life that can be described with these words. Intentionally think and meditate on these things. Reflect on these things as often as you can. After a few days, write down how this practice influenced your life.

3. What do we need to do to experience the peace of God being with us?

DAY THREE READING AND QUESTIONS

¹⁰ I rejoice greatly in the Lord that at last you have renewed your concern for me. Indeed, you have been concerned, but you had no opportunity to show it. ¹¹ I am not saying this because I am in need, for I have learned to be content whatever the circumstances. ¹² I know what it is to be in need, and I know what it is to have plenty. I have learned the secret of being content in any and every situation, whether well fed or hungry, whether living in plenty or in want. ¹³ I can do everything through him who gives me strength.

¹⁴ Yet it was good of you to share in my troubles. ¹⁵ Moreover, as you Philippians know, in the early days of your acquaintance with the gospel, when I set out from Macedonia, not one church shared with me in the matter of giving and receiving, except you only; ¹⁶ for even when I was in Thessalonica, you sent me aid again and again when I was in need. ¹⁷ Not that I am looking for a gift, but I am looking for what may be credited to your account. ¹⁸ I have received full payment and even more; I am amply supplied, now that I have received from Epaphroditus the gifts you sent. They are a fragrant offering, an acceptable sacrifice, pleasing to God. ¹⁹ And my God will meet all your needs according to his glorious riches in Christ Jesus.

1. For what was Paul thankful?

2. Upon what did Paul's contentment depend?

3. What was the benefit Paul received from the gift send to him by the Philippians?

DAY FOUR READING AND QUESTIONS

[20] To our God and Father be glory for ever and ever. Amen.

[21] Greet all the saints in Christ Jesus. The brothers who are with me send greetings. [22] All the saints send you greetings, especially those who belong to Caesar's household.

[23] The grace of the Lord Jesus Christ be with your spirit. Amen.

1. Why does Paul end in an ascription of praise to God?

2. What does Paul's greeting tell us about the spreading of the gospel?

3. What is "the grace" which Paul desires to be with us?

DAY FIVE READING AND QUESTIONS

Reread the entire text (4:2-23)

1. Do you know of contentions in your community of faith you might help resolve? If so, spend much time in prayer and then be God's minister of reconciliation.

2. Do you worry? If so, develop the practice of going to God in a prayer of thanksgiving for all he has provided you in the past.

3. How might we learn to be thankful for gifts as Paul was thankful? In other words, he was not thankful for what the gifts did for him

as much as what it did for the giver. How might this change our
attitude towards gifts received?

MEDITATION

Once again we come to the topic of the contented life. It is, I believe, the desire of every human heart. To live a life of meaning, purpose, and joy is what all seek—what philosophers call the *summum bonum* (life of ultimate goodness). Every significant teacher, spiritual leader or guru in history has provided their own interpretation of this. Every world religion attempts to lead its adherents to this. What is the true "good life?" For Paul, it is found in one word: Jesus. In him, you truly rejoice. In him, there is no place for anxiety. Can you imagine? In the place of worry one has the peace of God that stands as a sentinel to one's heart. It is a peace that surpasses anything any other possible story of life might promise to provide. In Jesus Christ, *summum bonum* is personified.

Paul provides one more rather surprising true life example of such peace. Indeed, he has found that "contented life." That is not what is surprising. Note how Paul handles the gift he has received from the Philippians. He is thankful for the love the gift demonstrates, but he never really thanks them for the gift itself. The truth is—he didn't need it. God used the Philippians to meet Paul's needs—but it was God provision. Paul was thankful for the credit they received for doing good in God's name—but Paul no longer had personal desires. Whatever the situation, he was content. His joy did not depend on outward circumstances. He did not live in that story of life. Rather, he had all he needed. He had found "the contented life." Rich, poor, oppressed, distressed, persecuted or comfortable, he was content. He invites us to find that life as well. "Rejoice in the Lord, always. I will say it again, rejoice!"

"Lord, may we find that life offered only in Jesus. A life of true meaning and joy, not based on our expectations, but rather on your promises."

COLOSSIANS:

LIVING IN THE CHRIST STORY

THE SPIRITUALITY OF COLOSSIANS

Paul's letter to the church at Colossae confronts a situation that is surprisingly relevant. While it is obvious that much has changed since Paul's writings, many of the principle challenges he addresses in this letter relate directly to us. Colossae, while a small town, had a wide diversity of life philosophies represented. Caesar was promoted as Lord, the Roman Empire as the provider of peace. There were traces of eastern religions, worship of angels, proponents of Judaism as well as elements of other philosophies of life. While today's mix of world religions and secular philosophies may be different, we face the same struggle of keeping our discipleship to Jesus uncontaminated by them.

We live in a world of competing framing stories. A framing story is a story that attempts to provide a true interpretation of the meaning of life. Every religion and philosophy of life is attempting to explain the purpose and direction of our lives. For this reason, we need to hear Paul's call to live according to the only true pattern of life (framing story)—Jesus Christ. Consider the following themes that address this concern:

UNCONTAMINATED DISCIPLESHIP

The main problem Paul confronts in this letter is sycretism—taking bits and pieces of various religious and social belief systems and combining them into a comfortable, practical concoction. Paul warns, "See to it that no one takes you captive through hollow and deceptive philosophy" (Colossians 2:8). I can't think of a message of greater importance for today's church. We are inundated with the constant noise of culture of consumerism, "Life is about having what you want." We find ourselves in the uncomfortable position of having one foot firmly planted in the secular world with the other reaching out for the kingdom of God. We need to hear Paul's passionate reminder—there is one true story of life and it is uncompromisingly true. Life can only be found in Christ Jesus. Paul's letter calls us to identify the idolatrous traces of other philosophies in our thinking and remove them so that we can be available to God for every good purpose.

THE CENTRALITY OF CHRIST JESUS

Colossians reminds us of the centrality of Christ in all things. All things were created by him, through him, for him, and he holds all things together! We affirm our belief in these truths through our baptism. Our submissive response to God's wonderful grace is a declaration of our desire to claim Christ Jesus as the only Lord of our lives. Because we have been raised with him, we must focus our lives on his concerns and on what he would do if he were in our place. Thus we are challenged to put to death whatever does not belong in a life wholly centered on Christ. Paul reminds us that our Christian walk is manifested through everything we do and say. It is demonstrated through every relationship. Paul calls us to ask, "Is Jesus Christ truly in the center of my life?"

KINGDOM LIVING

Colossians is a compelling reminder of the privilege we have been given to live in the kingdom of God. This message must not be watered down. Our allegiance to God's reign must not be compromised. We have "been given fullness in Christ" (2:10). The world has nothing to offer in comparison. Devoted to prayer, we are to keep our hearts, eyes, and ears open to the opportunities God provides to share the good news of life under his loving reign.

I have found Colossians to be a great help in presenting the essence of the gospel to "not yet Christians." In this brief letter, Paul tells us the wonderful story of life, reminds us of our personal commitment to its truth, and instructs us concerning how we should then live. Read his words to the Colossians with a deep desire to more fully realize the blessing of living in the Christ story!

"Lord, bless our study of this wonderful letter. May we recognize how little this world has to offer in comparison to your invitation to live in your kingdom! Through Jesus we pray, Amen."

THE TRUE STORY OF LIFE
(1:1-27)

DAY ONE READING AND QUESTIONS

¹ Paul, an apostle of Christ Jesus by the will of God, and Timothy our brother,

² To the holy and faithful brothers in Christ at Colossae:

Grace and peace to you from God our Father.

³ We always thank God, the Father of our Lord Jesus Christ, when we pray for you, ⁴ because we have heard of your faith in Christ Jesus and of the love you have for all the saints— ⁵ the faith and love that spring from the hope that is stored up for you in heaven and that you have already heard about in the word of truth, the gospel ⁶ that has come to you. All over the world this gospel is bearing fruit and growing, just as it has been doing among you since the day you heard it and understood God's grace in all its truth. ⁷ You learned it from Epaphras, our dear fellow servant, who is a faithful minister of Christ on our behalf, ⁸ and who also told us of your love in the Spirit.

1. For what does Paul thank God when he prays for the Colossians?

2. What is the fruit of which Paul speaks?

3. What did Paul mean by their understanding God's grace in all its truth? Do you understand God's grace? Is it bearing fruit in you?

DAY TWO READINGS AND QUESTIONS

⁹ For this reason, since the day we heard about you, we have not stopped praying for you and asking God to fill you with the knowledge of his will through all spiritual wisdom and understanding. ¹⁰ And we pray this in order that you may live a life worthy of the Lord and may please him in every way: bearing fruit in every good work, growing in the knowledge of God, ¹¹ being strengthened with all power according to his glorious might so that you may have great endurance and patience, and joyfully ¹² giving thanks to the Father, who has qualified you to share in the inheritance of the saints in the kingdom of light. ¹³ For he has rescued us from the dominion of darkness and brought us into the kingdom of the Son he loves, ¹⁴ in whom we have redemption, the forgiveness of sins.

> *1. If they already understood God's grace, why did Paul want them to have more knowledge?*

> *2. How do we gain endurance and patience according to Paul?*

> *3. In what sense were the Colossians "rescued?"*

DAY THREE READING AND QUESTIONS

¹⁵ He is the image of the invisible God, the firstborn over all creation. ¹⁶ For by him all things were created: things in heaven and on earth, visible and invisible, whether thrones or powers or rulers or authorities; all things were created by him and for him. ¹⁷ He is before all things, and in him all things hold together. ¹⁸ And he is the head of the body, the church; he is the beginning and the firstborn from among the dead, so that in everything he might have the supremacy. ¹⁹ For God was pleased to have all his fullness dwell in him, ²⁰ and through him to reconcile to himself all things, whether things on earth or things in heaven, by making peace through his blood, shed on the cross.

[21] Once you were alienated from God and were enemies in your minds because of your evil behavior. [22] But now he has reconciled you by Christ's physical body through death to present you holy in his sight, without blemish and free from accusation— [23] if you continue in your faith, established and firm, not moved from the hope held out in the gospel. This is the gospel that you heard and that has been proclaimed to every creature under heaven, and of which I, Paul, have become a servant.

> 1. *How does Paul describe Jesus Christ in verses 15 and 16? How does this impact you?*
>
> 2. *What is God doing through the blood of Jesus to this day?*
>
> 3. *In what sense were the Colossians once alienated from God and his enemies? What changed this?*

DAY FOUR READING AND QUESTIONS

[24] Now I rejoice in what was suffered for you, and I fill up in my flesh what is still lacking in regard to Christ's afflictions, for the sake of his body, which is the church. [25] I have become its servant by the commission God gave me to present to you the word of God in its fullness— [26] the mystery that has been kept hidden for ages and generations, but is now disclosed to the saints. [27] To them God has chosen to make known among the Gentiles the glorious riches of this mystery, which is Christ in you, the hope of glory.

> 1. *What did Paul mean by his suffering what was lacking in Christ's afflictions?*
>
> 2. *What was the mystery of God that Paul had been allowed to reveal?*

3. What is everyone's hope of glory? How is this realized?

DAY FIVE READING AND QUESTIONS

Reread the entire text (1:1-27)

1. Do you feel rescued from darkness and brought into God's kingdom? Why or why not?

2. Do you believe Paul's description of the supremacy of Christ? If so, how does this truth influence your daily life? How should it influence our lives?

3. Paul so closely identifies with Christ that he is willing to continue to suffer as needed for the cause of God. Can you say this with Paul? If not, why not?

MEDITATION

One of the wonderful characteristics of Paul's writings is his constant dialogue with God (prayers)– right in the middle of making a point to his readers. It is a great reminder to me to intentionally keep God involved in my conversations, whether spoken or written. Paul's opening prayer for the Colossian believers is one of my favorite. He desperately wants his brothers and sisters to grow in their knowledge of God's will through "spiritual wisdom and understanding." What a great description of "spiritual formation." As we grow in our understanding of God's will, we more fully experience the life for which we were created! We please the Lord, bear nutritious fruit to feed a hungry world, and we share in the inheritance of the kingdom of light! There is no greater offer in all of human history than this. We have been rescued from a meaningless life in the kingdom of darkness to shine as full participants in God's reign.

Paul's summary of the pinnacle of God's story for humanity is simply stunning. Colossians 1:15-22 would be a great passage to read every morning. If we believe it is true, it has to change everything in our lives. There is only one true story that adequately and accurately interprets all of history and this is it—Jesus, the Christ. He is before all things, through him all things were created, for him all things were created, and he holds it all together. Not only this, but God is at work today reconciling the world to himself through the blood of the cross. It is this story of life that gives us our identity as well as the direction for our daily lives. Before we embraced this story, we had no real purpose. We were alienated from God and therefore from life. Now, we have been given a new life and a reason to live that cannot be exhausted—no matter what happens to us in this world!

"Our loving Savior, help us see our lives in the context of your story of life. May we proclaim to all who know or encounter us that Jesus Christ is Lord and Savior."

BECOMING A PART OF THE CHRIST STORY

(1:28-2:23)

DAY ONE READING AND QUESTIONS

²⁸ We proclaim him, admonishing and teaching everyone with all wisdom, so that we may present everyone perfect in Christ. ²⁹ To this end I labor, struggling with all his energy, which so powerfully works in me.

²:¹ I want you to know how much I am struggling for you and for those at Laodicea, and for all who have not met me personally. ² My purpose is that they may be encouraged in heart and united in love, so that they may have the full riches of complete understanding, in order that they may know the mystery of God, namely, Christ, ³ in whom are hidden all the treasures of wisdom and knowledge. ⁴ I tell you this so that no one may deceive you by fine-sounding arguments. ⁵ For though I am absent from you in body, I am present with you in spirit and delight to see how orderly you are and how firm your faith in Christ is.

1. *What was Paul's stated purpose for writing this letter?*

2. *Where are all the treasures of wisdom and knowledge hidden? How do we access this?*

3. *What kind of "fine-sounding arguments" might mislead the believers from the truth that Jesus is the depository of all wisdom and knowledge?*

DAY TWO READING AND QUESTIONS

[6] So then, just as you received Christ Jesus as Lord, continue to live in him, [7] rooted and built up in him, strengthened in the faith as you were taught, and overflowing with thankfulness.

[8] See to it that no one takes you captive through hollow and deceptive philosophy, which depends on human tradition and the basic principles of this world rather than on Christ.

[9] For in Christ all the fullness of the Deity lives in bodily form, [10] and you have been given fullness in Christ, who is the head over every power and authority. [11] In him you were also circumcised, in the putting off of the sinful nature, not with a circumcision done by the hands of men but with the circumcision done by Christ, [12] having been buried with him in baptism and raised with him through your faith in the power of God, who raised him from the dead.

1. *How do we receive Christ Jesus as Lord? How, then, do we continue to live in him?*

2. *What are deceptive philosophies in our world today that depend on human tradition rather than Christ?*

3. *What does it mean to have been given fullness in Christ?*

DAY THREE READING AND QUESTIONS

[13] When you were dead in your sins and in the uncircumcision of your sinful nature, God made you alive with Christ. He forgave us all our sins, [14] having canceled the written code, with its regulations, that was against us and that stood opposed to us; he took it away, nailing it to the cross. [15] And having disarmed the powers and authorities, he made a public spectacle of them, triumphing over them by the cross.

[16] Therefore do not let anyone judge you by what you eat or drink, or with regard to a religious festival, a New Moon celebration or a Sabbath

day. [17] These are a shadow of the things that were to come; the reality, however, is found in Christ. [18] Do not let anyone who delights in false humility and the worship of angels disqualify you for the prize. Such a person goes into great detail about what he has seen, and his unspiritual mind puffs him up with idle notions. [19] He has lost connection with the Head, from whom the whole body, supported and held together by its ligaments and sinews, grows as God causes it to grow.

1. *Who makes us alive? Why is this necessary? (What was our condition before this action?)*

2. *What was nailed to the cross for our personal benefit? Who was disarmed as a result?*

3. *What effect should this truth (the accomplishment of the cross) have on our lives?*

DAY FOUR READING AND QUESTIONS

[20] Since you died with Christ to the basic principles of this world, why, as though you still belonged to it, do you submit to its rules: [21] "Do not handle! Do not taste! Do not touch!"? [22] These are all destined to perish with use, because they are based on human commands and teachings. [23] Such regulations indeed have an appearance of wisdom, with their self-imposed worship, their false humility and their harsh treatment of the body, but they lack any value in restraining sensual indulgence.

1. *How do we die with Christ to the basic principles of the world? What does this mean?*

2. *What is the problem with teachings such as "Do not handle! Do not taste! And so on?*

3. Why are these kinds of teachings ineffective on restraining our sensual indulgence?

DAY FIVE READING AND QUESTIONS

Reread the entire text (1:28-2:23)

1. Do you so value the message of life as it is revealed in Christ that nothing can distract you from its profound implications? If not, how can we deepen our appreciation of this revealed mystery of life?

2. Do you feel complete in Christ Jesus? If not, why not?

3. Have you experienced victory over the powers and authorities (Satan and his influence)? What can we do to more fully realize the power of the new life we have been given in Christ Jesus?

MEDITATION

In a world full of stories competing for our affection, how do we claim the story of Jesus as our own? Paul reminds us of the exclusive nature of this understanding of the purpose and design of life. I can think of no greater need than to hear Paul's warning, "See to it that no one takes you captive through hollow and deceptive philosophy." Any teaching concerning the nature of life that is not based on the life and teachings of Jesus is hollow and deceptive. Have you been led to believe that security can be found in material wealth? You have been deceived. Have you be led to believe well being can be found in wealth and worldly success? You have been deceived. There is only one true manifestation of life, and it is Jesus Christ.

We claimed that story as our own when we were baptized. All the fullness of God is in Christ, and we have received that fullness when we submitted our lives to the redemptive story of God. We were dead, hopeless, without identity when God made us alive with him by the same power that raised Jesus from the dead! We participated in the divine narrative of salvation when we were buried with Jesus in baptism. We have experienced resurrection with him through the power of God. Our sins cancelled, we now have new life in God's kingdom.

The story is too good to be true—but it is true. We have been made complete, brought to fullness in Christ Jesus. The world no longer has anything to offer us. Freed from the expectations of the world, we can now fully pursue God's purposes for our lives! All of this is caused by the action and the power of God. In our baptism, we participated in the saving grace of God by reenacting the drama of salvation. We were dead, buried, and then raised by the power of God. No other story of life deserves my allegiance. There is only one story, and it is Jesus Christ, Lord and Savior. As the old hymn reminds us, "This is my story, this is my song—praising my Savior all the day long!"

"Father, thank you for the gift of baptism. Thank you for the invitation to claim the story of Jesus as our story. Thank you for the saving power you so freely grant through the death, burial and resurrection of our Lord. May we not be deceived by any other philosophy or story about life. We acknowledge life is found only in submission to our Lord and Savior. We pray through his name, Amen."

DRESSING OURSELVES IN JESUS CHRIST

(3:1-4:1)

DAY ONE READING AND QUESTIONS

3:1 Since, then, you have been raised with Christ, set your hearts on things above, where Christ is seated at the right hand of God. 2 Set your minds on things above, not on earthly things. 3 For you died, and your life is now hidden with Christ in God. 4 When Christ, who is your life, appears, then you also will appear with him in glory.

5 Put to death, therefore, whatever belongs to your earthly nature: sexual immorality, impurity, lust, evil desires and greed, which is idolatry. 6 Because of these, the wrath of God is coming. 7 You used to walk in these ways, in the life you once lived. 8 But now you must rid yourselves of all such things as these: anger, rage, malice, slander, and filthy language from your lips. 9 Do not lie to each other, since you have taken off your old self with its practices 10 and have put on the new self, which is being renewed in knowledge in the image of its Creator. 11 Here there is no Greek or Jew, circumcised or uncircumcised, barbarian, Scythian, slave or free, but Christ is all, and is in all.

1. *What do you think Paul means when he calls us to set our hearts and minds on things above? How would that look, practically, in our day to day lives?*

2. *How are we to put to death that which is of earthly nature?*

3. What is the essence of the new self of which we are to clothe ourselves?

DAY TWO READING AND QUESTIONS

[12] Therefore, as God's chosen people, holy and dearly loved, clothe yourselves with compassion, kindness, humility, gentleness and patience. [13] Bear with each other and forgive whatever grievances you may have against one another. Forgive as the Lord forgave you. [14] And over all these virtues put on love, which binds them all together in perfect unity.

[15] Let the peace of Christ rule in your hearts, since as members of one body you were called to peace. And be thankful. [16] Let the word of Christ dwell in you richly as you teach and admonish one another with all wisdom, and as you sing psalms, hymns and spiritual songs with gratitude in your hearts to God. [17] And whatever you do, whether in word or deed, do it all in the name of the Lord Jesus, giving thanks to God the Father through him.

1. How are we to clothe ourselves with these attributes of Jesus? How do you think we are to do this?

2. How and why are we to forgive?

3. What does it mean to do everything in the name of the Lord Jesus?

DAY THREE READING AND QUESTIONS

[18] Wives, submit to your husbands, as is fitting in the Lord.

[19] Husbands, love your wives and do not be harsh with them.

[20] Children, obey your parents in everything, for this pleases the Lord.

[21] Fathers, do not embitter your children, or they will become discouraged.

1. To what behavior does Paul call wives?

2. To what behavior does Paul call husbands?

3. What is the relationship Paul calls for between parents and children?

DAY FOUR READING AND QUESTIONS

[22] Slaves, obey your earthly masters in everything; and do it, not only when their eye is on you and to win their favor, but with sincerity of heart and reverence for the Lord. [23] Whatever you do, work at it with all your heart, as working for the Lord, not for men, [24] since you know that you will receive an inheritance from the Lord as a reward. It is the Lord Christ you are serving. [25] Anyone who does wrong will be repaid for his wrong, and there is no favoritism.

[4:1] Masters, provide your slaves with what is right and fair, because you know that you also have a Master in heaven.

1. To what does Paul call slaves? Upon what does Paul base his request for such behavior?

2. What were masters to do for their slaves?

3. What application might there be in these verses for us in our vocations?

DAY FIVE READING AND QUESTIONS

Reread the entire text (3:1-4:1)

1. If Paul were to challenge you to put to death things that do not belong in your life, what would those things be? How might you begin putting those things to death?

2. *Start each day intentionally dressing your soul with the attributes of Jesus as you put on your physical clothes. Try this for a few days and journal your results.*

3. *How does being an authentic disciple of Jesus influence your daily relationships? If married, do you treat your spouse in a God-honoring way? Your children? Your boss? Your teachers?*

MEDITATION

It is the power and action of God that saves us. Paul leaves no room for discussion on this. Before salvation, we were dead in our sins. What can a dead person do to raise themselves? Nothing. Absolutely nothing. But God, through his grace and mercy, made us alive, raising us from the dead with Jesus, to live in the kingdom of light. Note that all the verbs in chapter two that deal with salvation are passive—meaning the action is from someone besides us. Paul begins chapter three with a reminder that the saving action is all from God, "Since, then, you have been raised..." We do not resurrect ourselves! However, we do have a responsibility in taking specific actions in order to fully realize the salvation given to us. We must now set our minds and hearts on the true story of life—on things above. And we must put to death any affections in our hearts that are earth-ward.

Here, again, is another passage that stresses the importance of the spiritual disciplines. There are disciplines in which we intentionally engage with God (study, prayer, meditation, spiritual equipping, for example) and disciplines where we intentionally separate ourselves from anything that is not of God. We are to put to death everything in our lives that does not pertain to the kingdom. Spend time meditating on this. What, in your life, is out of place with God's rule? Paul reminds the Colossians they used to live for those kinds of things before they knew the true story of life. Now they must get rid of those things, and so must we.

But the Christian faith is not just putting things away that do not belong. We are to intentionally dress ourselves in the character of Jesus. A good friend once taught me to dress my soul as I dress my body every morning. As you put on a particular item of clothing, think of a specific characteristic of Jesus—compassion, kindness, humility, and so on. Say it out loud. Make it real. Put it on. Then, whether it is your jacket or your final cup of coffee, make sure you put on the love of Jesus, which binds all things together. I have found this to be an extremely helpful exercise.

God is the one who graciously grants salvation. This is his work and his alone. But we are called to participate in living out its potential. Until we can say that everything we do, in word and deed, is done in the name (under the authority) of the Lord Jesus, we have work to do.

"God of grace, we thank you for your saving power and amazing mercy. Help us remove from our lives what does not belong. Remind us through your Spirit to intentionally clothe ourselves with the character of Jesus."

MAKING THE MOST OF EVERY OPPORTUNITY

(4:2-4:18)

DAY ONE READING AND QUESTIONS

[2] Devote yourselves to prayer, being watchful and thankful. [3] And pray for us, too, that God may open a door for our message, so that we may proclaim the mystery of Christ, for which I am in chains. [4] Pray that I may proclaim it clearly, as I should. [5] Be wise in the way you act toward outsiders; make the most of every opportunity. [6] Let your conversation be always full of grace, seasoned with salt, so that you may know how to answer everyone.

1. How does one devote oneself to prayer?

2. For what did Paul request his readers to pray on his behalf? Why?

3. What should be the nature of our conversation with "outsiders?"

DAY TWO READING AND QUESTIONS

[7] Tychicus will tell you all the news about me. He is a dear brother, a faithful minister and fellow servant in the Lord. [8] I am sending him to you for the express purpose that you may know about our circumstances and that he may encourage your hearts. [9] He is coming with Onesimus, our faithful and dear brother, who is one of you. They will tell you everything that is happening here.

1. How is Tychicus described? How would Paul describe you if he knew you?

2. What was Paul's purpose in sending Tychicus?

3. Who is Onesimus (see Philemon)?

DAY THREE READING AND QUESTIONS

[10] My fellow prisoner Aristarchus sends you his greetings, as does Mark, the cousin of Barnabas. (You have received instructions about him; if he comes to you, welcome him.) [11] Jesus, who is called Justus, also sends greetings. These are the only Jews among my fellow workers for the kingdom of God, and they have proved a comfort to me. [12] Epaphras, who is one of you and a servant of Christ Jesus, sends greetings. He is always wrestling in prayer for you, that you may stand firm in all the will of God, mature and fully assured. [13] I vouch for him that he is working hard for you and for those at Laodicea and Hierapolis. [14] Our dear friend Luke, the doctor, and Demas send greetings. [15] Give my greetings to the brothers at Laodicea, and to Nympha and the church in her house.

1. Do you remember Paul's last recorded encounter with Mark (see Acts 15:36-39)? What does this new mention of him tell you about Mark?

2. Why do you think Paul mentions that there are only a few Jews with him?

3. What do you think it means that Epaphras is "wrestling in prayer" for the Colossians? Is there anyone for whom you wrestle in prayer?

DAY FOUR READING AND QUESTIONS

[16] After this letter has been read to you, see that it is also read in the church of the Laodiceans and that you in turn read the letter from Laodicea.

[17] Tell Archippus: "See to it that you complete the work you have received in the Lord."

[18] I, Paul, write this greeting in my own hand. Remember my chains. Grace be with you.

1. *What does this reading tell us of how the various letters were circulated by the early churches?*

2. *What might Paul be challenging Archippus to complete?*

3. *Why does Paul emphasize he is writing the final greeting with his own hand?*

DAY FIVE READING AND QUESTIONS

Reread the entire text (4:2-18)

1. *If Paul were writing a letter from your church, who would be the saints he would mention by name because of their noble service?*

2. *How do Paul's personal greetings and messages affect you? If you tend to skim over them, stop and meditate about the reality of the relationships he mentions.*

3. *If Paul were to write to your friends and family and call you by name with the following message, "See to it that you complete the work you have received in the Lord," what would that work be?*

MEDITATION

The greatest evangelist of all time in the Christian church, most agree, was Paul. One cannot read his letters, or read of his life as recorded in Acts, and not be deeply impressed by his passion to share the good news of Jesus with the lost. Yet, he rarely discusses how this is to be done. Paul didn't offer evangelism seminars as he worked with churches. He taught about Jesus as Lord and Savior. I believed Paul assumed all would have a deep desire to share the story of Jesus with the unsaved.

Nonetheless, there are a couple of passages where Paul was pretty direct about one's behavior with nonbelievers. In 1 Corinthians, he spoke of being all things to all people so that he might save same. We now call this "audience oriented" evangelism—that is, identify fully with those you are teaching so that you are effective in bringing them to an understanding of Christ. While there are other thoughts Paul contributes concerning how to effectively reach out with the truth, this passage in Colossians is his most direct teaching on evangelistic methodology. It begins with something so basic it is sometimes forgotten, "Devote yourselves to prayer, be watchful and thankful." Would it be an overstatement to suggest that if all Christians would do just this (be devoted to prayer), it would radically change our effectiveness in reaching the world with the message of Jesus?

Paul understood he was not the one initiating the opportunities for reaching others with the gospel. That is why prayer is so important. It allows you to listen for God's voice and direction. God is the one who opens doors of opportunity to tell the story of Jesus. I am not suggesting we be passive and not attempt new ways to reach others. But I can tell you from my own experience in missions and church planting as well as listening to the stories of others that by far the greater work done was through doors of opportunity we never would have even considered. God was and is at work!

God loves his children. Every human is his child. Tragically, many don't know who they are. Those of us who do are to become responders to God's initiative to save all. And when those doors open, may we have the boldness to walk through them in faith. May our speech be a gift, a demonstration of the grace of God, slightly seasoned with tasty salt, so that we know how to answer everyone. I love the thought of our speech being flavored with salt. Paul here is encouraging us to seek ways of whetting one's appetite to know more. Too often we flood others with more than they want to know, ruining the opportunity to teach.

"Saving Lord, lover of all souls, teach us to seek the doors you open, and to prepare ourselves for the opportunities you provide to share the wonderful news of Jesus as Lord."

PHILEMON:

ACCEPTING ONE ANOTHER IN CHRIST

THE SPIRITUALITY OF PHILEMON

Philemon is unique among the letters of Paul in the New Testament. It is personal correspondence dealing with a specific issue. A runaway slave has been converted by Paul, and is being sent back to his Christian master. Paul wants Philemon to allow the slave Onesimus to return to his former work, not as a runaway, but as a brother.

We might question why Paul did not attack the slavery as an institution. Apparently, he saw no need to do so in that cultural setting. Paul understood that Christ resolved issues of status and oppression in another manner. In Christ, there was no longer those distinctions which separate us (Galatians 3:28)—all are one in Christ. That did not mean, for Paul, that all such structures should be dissolved. The solution Paul sought was not personal freedom as the ultimate good, but authentic discipleship to Jesus no matter what your social role or condition in life. Love as you are loved, and all such structures will be transformed by the power of God. This answer makes the gospel truly good news wherever it might go until history comes to an end. True life is not found in personal freedom, it is found through loving submission to God wherever we might be. This is what overcomes the world.

There is much to learn from this brief letter. Note Paul's love for all involved. Pay attention to Paul's willingness to be intimately involved in the reconciliation of these brothers. Learn the discipline of approaching all conflicts with the commitment to love with God's love, and call those in the dispute to respond in love. Choose to believe that God is working through all circumstances of life, even those which bring us the most pain. Meditate on Paul's words carefully with an open heart.

"Lord, teach us to see the difficult situations we encounter through your eyes. Give us wisdom and courage to be used by you as ministers of reconciliation."

GREETINGS, THANKSGIVING, AND A PLEA

(1-14)

DAY ONE READING AND QUESTIONS

[1] Paul, a prisoner of Christ Jesus, and Timothy our brother,

To Philemon our dear friend and fellow worker, [2] to Apphia our sister, to Archippus our fellow soldier and to the church that meets in your home:

[3] Grace to you and peace from God our Father and the Lord Jesus Christ.

1. In what sense is Paul a prisoner?

2. Of what can we learn concerning the church in this brief reading?

3. What does it mean to live in the grace and peace that comes from God?

DAY TWO READING AND QUESTIONS

[4] I always thank my God as I remember you in my prayers, [5] because I hear about your faith in the Lord Jesus and your love for all the saints. [6] I pray that you may be active in sharing your faith, so that you will have a full understanding of every good thing we have in Christ. [7] Your love has given me great joy and encouragement, because you, brother, have refreshed the hearts of the saints.

1. For what is Paul thankful and prayerful?

2. Why is Paul prayerful that his readers be active in sharing their faith? What does Paul see resulting from such sharing?

3. How has Philemon's love brought Paul joy?

DAY THREE READING AND QUESTIONS

[8] Therefore, although in Christ I could be bold and order you to do what you ought to do, [9] yet I appeal to you on the basis of love. I then, as Paul—an old man and now also a prisoner of Christ Jesus— [10] I appeal to you for my son Onesimus, who became my son while I was in chains. [11] Formerly he was useless to you, but now he has become useful both to you and to me.

1. Why do you think Paul appeals to Philemon on the basis of love rather than command?

2. Why does Paul mention his age and condition?

3. What do you think Paul means when he said Onesimus became his son while in chains? Why would this now make him useful?

DAY FOUR READING AND QUESTIONS

[12] I am sending him—who is my very heart—back to you. [13] I would have liked to keep him with me so that he could take your place in helping me while I am in chains for the gospel. [14] But I did not want to do anything without your consent, so that any favor you do will be spontaneous and not forced.

1. Why did Paul send Onesimus back to Philemon?

2. What could Onesimus have done that would have been more helpful to Paul?

3. What might Paul hope Philemon does with Onesimus once he is returned to Philemon?

DAY FIVE READING AND QUESTIONS

Reread the entire text (1-14)

1. How has sharing the gospel with others influenced your faith? Has it made you stronger in the Lord?

2. Have you found love or force to be the greater motivator? How so?

3. Why do you think Paul is so careful not to impose his will on Philemon? What might we learn from Paul's attitude?

MEDITATION

To say the least, this letter confronts a sensitive situation. Paul dearly loves Philemon, who had been legally wronged. Paul had come to dearly love Onesimus, who acted against Philemon. This was a very real and complex dilemma. Onesimus was a runaway slave. As he ran away, somehow he encountered Paul, and had been converted to Christ Jesus. Nonetheless, there still existed legal issues that had to be handled appropriately. What can we learn from this?

It is easy to lose ourselves in the question of why Paul did not attack directly the institution of slavery. After all, how could Philemon, a believer, own slaves? But such a question is not helpful in applying Paul's instruction in this letter to our present day lives. Likely the best answer to the question of slavery is that calling for the freedom of all slaves simply was not feasible in Paul's day. However, whatever inequities, whatever oppression existed, Paul knew how to resolve the issue between Onesimus and Philemon. Because they were now brothers, Jesus Christ had taken care of the enmity between them. This is the lesson we need to learn from this situation. One's personal rights are not the most important thing according the gospel. The highest good is the love of Christ Jesus in us, and the love and forgiveness this provides for all our relationships. That calls us to behaviors our worldly society will never understand. Philemon had been wronged. No question. Onesimus had violated the legal rights of Philemon. If we can forget the issue of slavery for a moment, we suddenly have a very relevant issue. One brother has wronged another. What should be done?

Is there anyone in your past or present who has wronged you? If Paul were to address you in a personal letter, what do you think he would ask of you? If Jesus were to speak to you personally about that which has caused discord between you and that person, what do you think he would advise you to do?

"Dear God of forgiveness, teach us to love and forgive."

NO LONGER A SLAVE, BUT A BROTHER

(15-25)

DAY ONE READING AND QUESTIONS

[15] Perhaps the reason he was separated from you for a little while was that you might have him back for good— [16] no longer as a slave, but better than a slave, as a dear brother. He is very dear to me but even dearer to you, both as a man and as a brother in the Lord.

1. When bad things happen, do you look for the good that results? Why or why not?

2. What does Paul suggest might be the reason for Onesimus running away?

3. Why does Paul describe Onesimus as a "dear" brother?

DAY TWO READING AND QUESTIONS

[17] So if you consider me a partner, welcome him as you would welcome me. [18] If he has done you any wrong or owes you anything, charge it to me. [19] I, Paul, am writing this with my own hand. I will pay it back—not to mention that you owe me your very self.

1. How does Paul want Philemon to receive Onesimus?

2. *What is Paul willing to do to make things right between Onesimus and Philemon?*

3. *Why does Paul remind Philemon of what he himself owes Paul? Is this an appropriate reminder? Why or why not?*

DAY THREE READING AND QUESTIONS

[20] I do wish, brother, that I may have some benefit from you in the Lord; refresh my heart in Christ. [21] Confident of your obedience, I write to you, knowing that you will do even more than I ask.

[22] And one thing more: Prepare a guest room for me, because I hope to be restored to you in answer to your prayers.

1. *How could Philemon refresh Paul?*

2. *What is the anticipated "more" that Paul awaits?*

3. *For what is Philemon to be prepared?*

DAY FOUR READING AND QUESTIONS

[23] Epaphras, my fellow prisoner in Christ Jesus, sends you greetings. [24] And so do Mark, Aristarchus, Demas and Luke, my fellow workers.
[25] The grace of the Lord Jesus Christ be with your spirit.

1. *Why do you think Paul closes his letters with personal greetings?*

2. *What does Paul closing greeting tell us about his situation?*

3. *Why does Paul call for the grace of the Lord to be with Philemon's "spirit"?*

DAY FIVE READING AND QUESTIONS

Reread the entire text (15-25)

1. Can you think of a time in your life when something went very wrong, but it ended up bringing great blessings? If so, do you think God was involved in the blessing being given?

2. Have you ever attempted to resolve conflicts between believers? What can we learn from Paul concerning conflicts between friends?

3. Ultimately, what do you think Philemon did? Why?

MEDITATION

One might call it manipulative language. It sure seems Paul was using everything at his disposal to make certain Philemon would warmly embrace Onesimus on his return. In fact, it's pretty clear Paul intended Philemon to free Onesimus, though Paul's language concerning this matter was carefully chosen (see verse 21). What perhaps is most valuable for us in this situation was Paul's heart for the reconciliation of believers. We might be more effective in our attempts to resolve conflict if we would follow Paul's example.

Note Paul's deep love for both parties in the conflict. His profound affection was what led him to seek their reconciliation. Do we love those involved in conflict as Paul loved? Motivated by love, Paul begged Philemon to respond in love. This brief letter is saturated in love. Philemon was greeted with love. Paul had received the love of Philemon and was deeply thankful for it. Onesimus was sent back to Philemon in love. If financial wrongs were suffered by Philemon, Paul so loved Onesimus that he was willing to pay for those damages himself. Paul pleaded with Philemon to love Onesimus as he had loved

Paul—embracing him as if he were Paul. Paul was clearly deeply invested in both Onesimus and Philemon. How could Philemon respond other than in generous love?

As world history continues to be written and experienced, new situations of conflict will arise. Cultural norms may dictate what can be done legally with conflicts, but if both parties are disciples of Jesus, the means to reconciliation will never change. We are called to love one another. So, whether you are the one attempting to resolve a conflict between brothers and sisters in Christ, or, you are one involved in conflict, saturate your attempt to resolve the issue in love. In so doing, you put Christ Jesus above all. Everything and everyone else pales in comparison. Love as you are loved. God is glorified and the grace of the Lord Jesus Christ will indeed be with your spirit.

" Lord above all lords, King above all kings, rule our hearts so that we will love others as you love us, and will glorify God, our father in all we do and say."

The Meditative Commentary Series

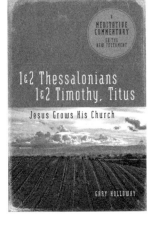
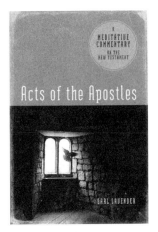
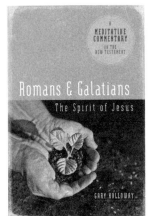
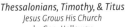
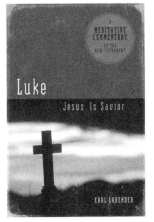
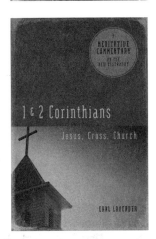

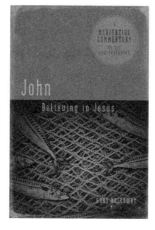

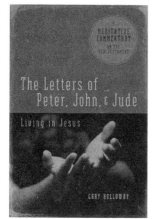